Parents' Guide to Creating Wonderful People

Parents' Guide to Creating Wonderful People

How to Help Your Children
Grow Up to Live
Happy and Meaningful Lives

by Jennifer Berryman, Ph.D.

LANGMARC
PUBLISHING
AUSTIN, TEXAS

Parents' Guide to Creating Wonderful People

How to Help Your Children
Live Happy and Meaningful Lives
By Jennifer Berryman, Ph.D.

Cover by Michael Qualben
Copyright © 2011 by Jennifer Berryman
First printing 2011
Printed in the United States of America

Published by LangMarc Publishing
P.O. 90488
Austin, Texas 78709
www.langmarc.com

ISBN: 1-880292-43-2
Library of Congress Control number: 2011940650

DEDICATION

To my husband, Mark,
and our wonderful daughters,
Rachel and Megan
(Their pictures appear on the front cover.
Megan is riding the horse and
Rachel is posing for a prom picture
with Alexander Grant.)

CONTENTS

PREFACE

Raising children is such a major part of every parent's life. Our role begins the moment we hold our first child and does not end when our last child grows up and moves away. We want to be great parents, but what does that mean and what is it that we're really trying to accomplish?

Although the answers will vary, most of us would probably say that we're hoping to have a loving relationship with our children, one that will last a lifetime. We see ourselves sharing in our children's joy, being there for them during the tough times, and helping them grow up to be wonderful people. We want to raise children who will be successful, but we also want them to become happy, loving, and compassionate adults. We want to prepare our children to handle the stressors they'll inevitably face in life, teach them values so that they grow up to be respectable members of society, help them find meaning in life, and show them how to form healthy, loving relationships.

We know what we want to accomplish, but we'd be lying if we didn't admit that we're all a little nervous when it comes to parenting. Being a parent is an extremely difficult job and creating great people is an overwhelming responsibility.

Most of us have questions and are looking for answers. For example, how do we help our children develop good values or give them the skills they need to cope with stressors such as the death of a loved one, academic failure, or teasing from peers? What's the best way to teach them how to express their emotions, develop a strong sense of self, retain their love of learning, and develop the skills they'll need to be successful and happy in today's world? Most importantly, what can we do to help our children form healthy relationships and find meaning in life?

This isn't a book about how to use time-out effectively or to get your children to complete their homework. Instead, it's designed to teach you how to use your relationship with your children to help them grow up to be exceptional people.

This book is written for parents who were fortunate enough to be raised in loving homes and by great parents, as well parents who hope to do a better job at parenting than their own parents did. It's a book for people who take their role as a parent seriously and want to do everything possible to give their children a great childhood and strong foundation to build upon.

Jennifer Berryman

ACKNOWLEDGMENTS

I am incredibly grateful to my family for all of their support and assistance. Mark has not only been a great husband and father, but he was incredibly patient and supportive as I spent several years writing this book. My daughters, Rachel and Megan, provided endless help and encouragement as I worked on this project and have made being a mother so much more rewarding than I ever imagined it would be. I couldn't have asked for better children, and I'm very proud of them. They are truly wonderful people.

Much thanks goes to Lois Qualben, president of LangMarc Publishing, for making the process of publishing a book so enjoyable and to Beth Sulzer-Azaroff, June Groden, Patti DiNardo, and David Paul Smith for taking the time to review it. Their feedback was invaluable.

And special thanks to Hannah May Henry for allowing me to use her photo of Megan riding.

Finally, I want to thank my friends who quietly supported and encouraged me as I talked endlessly about my desire to publish a book. They knew how important it was for me to find a creative outlet where I could have a positive impact on others and encouraged me to make that happen.

Chapter 1

Attention

All you have to do is sit by a pool full of young children, stand near a slide at a playground, or watch an elementary school play to know how important attention is for children. Kids inevitably will yell, "Mom, watch!" as they do a cannonball into the pool or go down the slide or wave to Dad from up on the stage in the middle of the kindergarten play.

When my kids were little, I was always amazed at how they could play independently at my feet, but the minute I picked up a book or newspaper they demanded my undivided attention. When I told my friends who had older children about my observation, their answers were always basically the same: "Oh I remember those days. I don't think I read a book for at least five or six years back then."

As much as we love to spend time with our children, sometimes their need for attention can be exhausting, especially if we're tired or had a stressful day at work.

We want to give our children the attention they deserve, but we know we won't do a very good job of that if we don't take care of our needs, too. It's perfectly normal and healthy for adults to want time away from their kids to relax, read a book without being interrupted or interact with other adults. Most of us understand, though, that raising children is a time-consuming task and that children need to have attention from a supportive caregiver if they are going to grow up to be happy, secure adults.

What happens to children who don't get the attention they need? Many grow up with a void inside of them, a feeling that they're not important, and they sense a need that can't be fulfilled. Some adults who lacked adequate attention as children will try to fill the void by becoming clingy and dependent in relationships. Others will demand to be the center of attention at all times and have difficulty sharing the spotlight with others.

We all know people like that, those who monopolize meetings in order to get the most attention from the boss or annoy friends by always talking about themselves and not listening to others. Their one-sided relationships may work for a while but in the end they backfire, leaving these people feeling lonely and depressed.

Some people try to fill their emptiness with food, alcohol or drugs, and many spend a lifetime feeling worthless or insecure. Fortunately, if you are a nurturing and attentive parent, your children are likely to grow up to become happy and secure adults.

Facts about Attention

Most children need a tremendous amount of attention from their parents. I was finishing graduate school when I was pregnant with Rachel, my first child. I told my friends that I was looking forward to taking a maternity leave. "It will give me time to finish my dissertation. I'm sure she'll sleep a lot and that will give me plenty of time to work on it." I remember that they just laughed. It wasn't until Rachel was born I realized how clueless I had been.

Sometimes parents don't realize how much attention children need because their parents didn't pay much attention to them. Adults who grew up in dysfunctional homes often experienced a great deal of neglect as children. They may have tried to avoid an alcoholic parent or had a father who was absent or were raised by an inattentive mother. They lacked good role models and have difficulty providing adequate attention to their children.

If you're one of these people, think about those folks in your life who did pay attention to you such as a favorite teacher, caring aunt, or nurturing neighbor. You may be able to use them as role models to help you successfully parent your own children. You may also want to seek additional help. Many people benefit from going to therapy, parenting classes, or a family resource center.

We owe it to our children to give them the amount of attention they require. When we decide to become parents, we become responsible for our children's growth and development and need to put forth our best efforts. Often that means we have to set aside our own wants in order to meet the needs of our children.

Children who do not receive enough attention will likely face more challenges than necessary in life. No one wants her child to become a sad, depressed, lonely or insecure adult. Life is difficult enough, and it's very important to give children a strong, secure foundation so they can handle the challenges they will inevitably face. Giving your kids the attention they need is one of the greatest gifts you can give them.

Absent parents can still give their children attention. Whenever possible, parents need to spend time with their children, but attention is not an all-or-nothing thing. If you live across the country, you can pay attention to your child by calling him and asking him how his day went or letting him know that you posted his swim schedule on the refrigerator so that you don't forget when he has a competition. Modern technology has made it easier for parents to stay involved in their children's lives. If you are a parent who doesn't live near your children, you can ask them to post video on the Internet and then talk with them about it on the phone while you're watching it. Living a long ways from your children is not ideal, but if you're creative you can still play an important role in your child's life. Frequent phone calls, texts, and e-mails give your children the message that you care about them.

Kids know when parents aren't giving them their undivided attention. You can't be attentive to your children if while you're interacting with them you're also talking on the phone, answering e-mails, or watching TV unless, of course, you and your children are doing that together. When you watch your children at their practices, games, and events, it's okay to talk with other adults, but remember why you're there. Children feel disappointed when their parents spend more time socializing with peers than watching them.

Don't worry. If you're not doing a good job paying attention to your children, they'll let you know. Young children will cry, pull on your pant leg, or tell you to look at them. Older kids will ask you if you're listening or say things like "Will you look at me when I'm talking?" or "Turn off the TV. I want to show you something." Kids are just like us. When you are paying attention to them, they want you to maintain eye contact, listen attentively, show an interest in what they're doing and seem genuinely happy to be spending time with them.

Babies require constant attention when they're awake. They need you to hold, cuddle, play with, smile at, and talk to them. That's how they develop an attachment to you, feel secure, and develop language skills. I cringe when parents say that they leave their babies crying in the crib to prevent them from becoming "spoiled." Babies don't get spoiled and repeated ignoring can cause them to feel frightened and depressed. It teaches them that their efforts to get attention aren't effective. Eventually they may stop trying to have their needs met, something parents certainly don't want to do to their children.

Older children need to learn that other people need attention, too. They need to hear that they aren't the only person in the world and to learn sometimes they have to wait because Mom has other demands for her attention or that it's not their turn to receive attention. Learning to delay gratification is an important skill that takes children years to learn. You can help your children learn to share attention by using clear communication such as "I'd love to read with you, but right now I have to finish dinner. We'll read that book before you go to bed." Or "Your brother went to your game yesterday. You need to go and watch him today. He likes the family to be there as much as you do."

Make sure you pay attention to your children's feelings as much as you pay attention to their actions and words. One of the best ways for kids to learn how to identify their emotions is to comment on what you see and ask them if your observations are correct. For example, you could say, "You're quieter than usual today, and you look a little sad. Are you feeling sad because Josh doesn't want to play with you?" It's easier to notice behaviors than emotions, but usually emotions are the key to problems. For example, an aggressive kid may actually be feeling sad but not be able to express his feelings in words.

Avoid becoming defensive if your children tell you that you aren't providing enough attention. Listen to them, take their concerns seriously, and try to do better in the future. We all get busy. Don't think there's a parent on earth who hasn't had times when they weren't as attentive to their children as they wish they had been. Don't be afraid to apologize to your children and take responsibility for your lack of attention. Kids need to see parents behaving in the same way they're expected to act. Don't be afraid to say, "I'm sorry, Honey. I was tired and hungry when you were talking to me about your day. I should have told you that I would be able to listen better after dinner." Or "You're right. I need to turn off the computer and listen to you."

Failing to pay adequate attention to your children can be dangerous and even life threatening. You can child proof your home, but you can't make it totally free of danger. Covering electrical outlets will prevent toddlers from sticking their fingers in them but won't prevent them from chewing on the cord and getting a shock.

Talking to your elementary school-aged children about the importance of not getting into cars with strangers won't guarantee that a sex offender can't persuade them to go with him and help him look for his lost puppy. Even teens need us to pay attention to them. Know where they're going, who's with them, and what they're doing. As they grow older, they can be given more independence but they still require parental supervision, especially in today's computer age.

Appreciate the fact that your child wants your attention. Don't be annoyed that your children value your attention so highly. Life isn't about the things you own. It's about having meaningful relationships with the people you love. Believe me, in no time your children will be grown, and you'll wish you could relive those days when they wanted to sit on your lap and read a book with you or show you every new skill they've developed.

Make sure you pay attention to healthy, positive behaviors. If you pay attention to your child only when he's sick, he may begin to constantly complain of headaches, stomachaches, or nausea. If you look up from your book or interact with your child only to correct her behavior, she is likely to act out even more.

Don't get me wrong. I'm not saying that you shouldn't pay attention to your children when they're sick or should ignore them when they're hitting other kids or being destructive. What I am saying is that the amount of attention you give to healthy, positive behaviors should far exceed the amount you give to negative behaviors. If you reprimand your child for being aggressive, make a conscious effort to praise him when he's playing nicely with his peers.

Questions to Ponder

Take a minute and ask yourself, *"Am I giving my children enough attention?"*
- If not, what's preventing you from doing so and what can you do to improve the situation?
- Do you think you pay enough attention to your children when they're doing good things or are you

so busy, tired, or stressed that you respond only when they're misbehaving?

* Is there a way you could remind yourself to focus more attention on their positive behaviors?
* How can you change your life so you can pay more attention to your children? Do you need to reduce your stress, ask for more help from your spouse, or maybe say "no" more often when people make demands on you?

Now think about your own childhood.

* Did your parents give you enough attention when you were growing up?
* If so, what did they do or say that made your feel special?
* If not, what prevented them from doing so? Were they drinking, seriously ill, suffering from a mental illness, depressed, or too self-centered to meet the needs of others including you?
* Were there other people in your life who nurtured you and gave you the attention you needed?
* If your parents were inattentive, how can you insure that you provide your children with the attention they need and don't follow in your parents' footsteps?

CHAPTER 2

A SENSE OF SELF

One of the most rewarding parts of parenting is helping your children develop into happy, interesting, and well-adjusted adults. Even when your children are very young, you'll discover that each of them has a unique personality. If you have more than one child, you will notice differences in temperament, interests, and talents.

Your children will be similar to you in some ways but very different in others. For example, if you and your husband are engineers, you may notice that your daughter shares your proclivity for detail. She may excel in math and dream of following in your footsteps. Your next child may be very different. He may have attention problems and a math learning disability but excel in sports and love the outdoors. You'll scratch your head wondering how you and your husband managed to produce the captain of the high school football team, a conservationist, or hiking guide.

Children figure out who they are by trying out different roles and participating in a range of activities. Somehow they manage to begin this process without much assistance from adults. We don't have to teach children how to pretend to be parents, doctors, or firefighters or how to use our pots and pans to make music or to build houses out of refrigerator boxes. Children and adolescents love to learn new skills, discover their strengths and talents, and dream about what career they'll have when they grow up. As parents, we can help them develop a strong sense of self by giving them opportunities to join clubs, attend camps, interact with a wide range of people, take lessons, and participate in sports.

Facts about Helping Children Develop a Strong Sense of Self

Encourage your children to use their imaginations. Many children don't have enough opportunities to use their imaginations, engage in unstructured play, or pursue their own interests because they spend too much time either in organized activities or using the computer, playing video games, texting, or watching TV.

Don't get me wrong. I am not opposed to children using technology or watching TV. These activities certainly have their benefits. For example, because of social networking sites, kids today have large networks of friends, and when they grow up they will have potentially hundreds of contacts for jobs that none of us had when we entered the job market. Educational shows have taught our kids about everything from global warming to the history of China, and the hours our children have spent on the computer have resulted in their learning computer skills most adults have never mastered. It's important for our kids to become proficient with technology, but it shouldn't dominate their lives.

Encourage your children to use their imaginations by creating art projects, playing dress up, writing stories, directing plays with neighborhood kids or building forts in the backyard. Ask them to turn off the TV, go outside and ride bikes, shoot baskets, or play tag.

Expose your children to a wide range of activities. Happy, successful people are well rounded. They enjoy many hobbies and can carry on conversations with people who have a variety of interests. Children love to experience new things and often will try just about anything at least once. This process helps them to learn what they enjoy and where their strengths and weaknesses lie. It's how they develop a sense of self.

Your son may not realize that he has a great sense of humor and a sharp wit until he takes a comedy workshop. Or your daughter may not be aware that she has great potential as a leader until she spends several weeks at camp where she has an opportunity to lead group activities. Encourage your children to step out of their comfort zones and try new things. That will help them develop new interests, as well as courage and confidence.

Don't worry if you don't have a lot of money to pay for lessons and educational opportunities. Most programs have at least a few scholarships available for children in need. Many provide fund-raising opportunities and encourage kids to pay for some, if not all, of the cost of the activity on their own.

In the past, young people never would have dreamed of being able to raise enough money to send themselves to Australia, lease a horse at a local barn, or pay for a theatre workshop on their own, but such opportunities may be within the reach of many children today. They sell candy and gifts, sponsor spaghetti suppers, and collect donations from friends and relatives. Many stable owners allow youngsters to work to pay for lessons or lease horses; art and music instructors might allow kids to baby-sit or do odd jobs in exchange for their lessons. If your child really wants to participate in a program, encourage her to raise some of the money herself. This will help her become self-reliant, give her a sense of accomplishment, and show her that she has the ability to reach her goals and get what she wants in life.

Encourage your children to stick with new activities until they have had the opportunity to become somewhat proficient at them. Most activities aren't much fun until you gain a minimal level of proficiency. Playing the piano is more enjoyable when you can actually play a song. Skiing is more appealing when you can ski down the hill without falling. Riding horses is more pleasurable when you can finally jump small fences and canter around the ring. Young people need to learn it takes time and practice to become good at something and that the effort can be very rewarding in the end.

Of course, if you're asking your child to make a commitment, you'll need to be willing to make one as well. If you register your daughter for dance class, plan on paying for lessons and driving her to the classes for the whole year so she can perform in the recital. If your son wants to play little league, you'll need to see to his transportation to practices and attend his games.

When your children join teams, encourage them to complete a season so they don't let their teammates down. Team activities and sports are great ways for kids to learn to work cooperatively with others, gain a sense of belonging, bond with other children, and learn about their strengths and weaknesses. It's also a terrific way for them to learn to follow through on commitments, a skill they'll certainly need as adults. If your kids join teams, insist they attend practices and go to all the games even if they're just sitting on the bench. *Don't force your children to stay in an activity that seems to be emotionally or physically damaging.* Commitment is important, but activities should improve your children's self-esteem, not damage it. If your child seems depressed or sad when you pick him up from an activity, ask him about it. If the coach or instructor is belittling him or is too punitive, either encourage your child to speak up for himself or talk with the coach for him. If the problem continues, allow your child to quit. Tell him that, although you believe he should follow through on commitments, no one should remain in a situation where they feel they aren't being treated with respect. Stress the importance of attempting to resolve conflicts, but explain to him that problems can't be resolved unless both parties are willing to compromise.

Ensure that coaches, trainers, or teachers share values that are consistent with those you want to teach your children. Occasionally your child may have a coach or instructor who doesn't share your values. You should give your children the message that people do have different perspectives, and we need to respect those differences, but it's important not to waiver when it comes to certain values. For example, I won't tolerate coaches or instructors who make racist remarks, devalue and demean children, condone cheating, or place them in dangerous situations. I've told my children that I will attempt to resolve disagreements with instructors, but I will take them out of activities if the coaches continue to encourage cheating, are mean to kids, or put them at risk.

Let your children choose the activities they like, not the ones you like. We all have interests we secretly hope our children will choose to pursue. Maybe you were a star football player and always dreamed that your son would be an even better player than you were. Or perhaps you were born with two left feet and always hoped your daughter would become a great ballerina, a goal you knew you could never attain. Sometimes we want our children to participate in activities such as theater, music, or sporting events just because we enjoy them. There's nothing wrong with that as long as your child enjoys those activities as well. The problem comes into play when parents try to live their lives through their children. It's too late for you to relive your childhood, and you certainly can't and shouldn't try to use your child to satisfy your own desires and needs.

Encourage your children to learn about people from other cultures, races, and socio-economic groups. One of the best ways for kids to figure out who they are and what they believe in is to compare themselves to others. This helps them to question their views and may result in their adopting some new perspectives and feeling more strongly about some ideas they already have. This is an important part of growing up and is a process that hopefully will continue throughout your child's life.

Talk with your children about their likes and dislikes, strengths, weaknesses, and values. Your children will change their views as they're growing up. Give them space to entertain different thoughts, try on different roles, and become more independent. As they begin to branch out on their own, they'll make mistakes just like you did. That's a normal part of growing up. (Of course, you should always intervene if you think your child is becoming involved in something illegal or dangerous. Don't sit back and watch your child develop a drug addiction, ride in cars with reckless drivers, hang out with kids who steal, associate with gangs, or engage in violent behavior.)

Encourage your children to dream big and to set high goals for themselves. After all, there are kids who go on to win gold medals in the Olympics, become president, manage highly successful companies, and develop non-profits that impact large numbers of people around the world. Encourage your kids to set the bar high, and then help them work to attain that goal by finding them good role models for success, giving them opportunities to develop the skills they will need to reach their goals, and providing them with support and encouragement.

When I was a growing up, many kids in my town rode horses and competed in horse shows. Most of our parents were supportive but saw our riding as a hobby that would end when we left for college. One family was a little different. They encouraged their daughter to set high goals and supported her efforts to reach them. She's all grown up now and continues to ride. Not only did she make riding her career, she went on to win numerous Olympic medals in equestrian events. You never know. Your kids might just surprise you by accomplishing amazing things.

Provide opportunities for your children to clarify their values. Much of our sense of self comes from our values. We are not just a parent, spouse, or professional. We have values such as honesty, integrity, hard work, and compassion. We have political views and perspectives on religion. We differ in how much emphasis we place on status, money, material goods, protecting the environment, giving to others, relationships, and traditions, to name just a few of the factors that shape who we are. It's important to remember that your children may share many of your beliefs, but they won't share all of them, just as you don't see eye to eye on all issues with your parents.

Initially your children will learn their values from you and other adults in their lives. But as they mature, that will change and their peer group will play a greater role in defining who they become. That's a normal part of growing up and a reality that all parents, sadly, have to learn to accept.

Keep the avenues of communication open as your children figure out who they are. Let your children know they can talk to you about whatever is bothering them, even if those discussions make you uncomfortable. Remember, no one ever said being a parent is easy.

Sometimes children want to talk about topics some parents find difficult to discuss such as sexual orientation and gender identity. Many people in our current generation are more open to homosexuality issues than our parents were. But I think it's fair to say that hardly any parent wants to know that his son feels like he should be a girl or a daughter is convinced she is really a boy in a girl's body. Kids with gender identity problems face challenges in life none of us want our children to have to endure. If your children are struggling with these issues, educate yourself as much as possible about them and consider joining a support group or talking with a therapist who specializes in these issues.

Adults who are gay, lesbian, bisexual, or transgender usually say that their sexual orientation or gender identity was not a choice for them but reflects who they are. They report feeling different from other kids at a very early age and wishing they had been able to talk openly about this with their parents. Let your children know you are always there for them and that no topic, no matter how difficult it is to discuss, is off limits.

Encourage your adolescents to work. Many of us are more financially secure than our parents were and better able to provide for our children. Be careful if that is the case with you. It's great to be able to give our children opportunities to travel, attend camps, or buy the latest technology, but we need to be careful not to deprive them of the opportunity to work. Jobs help kids identify their strengths and weaknesses and teach them the value of money, how to budget, and the importance of hard work. Working helps adolescents move out of the role of a child, something everyone needs to do in order to become a well-adjusted adult. Jobs can help your kids learn responsibility, integrity, and honesty and realize the world doesn't revolve around them.

Be careful not to use one or two traits or characteristics to define your children. This is particularly important if your child has an illness or handicapping condition. Over the years, people have changed the language they use to describe people in order to prevent this from occurring. For example, it's no longer politically correct to say that children are retarded. Instead, we refer to them as children with developmental disabilities. It may sound like a minor detail, but it really isn't. We need to remember they are children who happen to have cognitive deficits. They are also children who may love animals, have a delightful sense of humor, enjoy going for walks with family members, etc. This is very important if your child has a serious illness, learning disability, or physical or mental disorder.

If your child has one of these challenges, try to teach her that it is just one part of who she is and not her whole identity. Try to keep her life as normal as possible, focus on her strengths rather than weaknesses and ensure that she has opportunities to have quality relationships, learn skills, and have as much fun as every other kid.

Help your child integrate her disability into her sense of self. For example, explain to her that although she has a physical disability she also is great in math, she is a dependable friend and a wonderful daughter. Remind her there's no such thing as a perfect person or a perfect life. Explain to her that everyone faces challenges in life. Some kids are poor, live in dangerous neighborhoods, and have serious health problems, while others struggle to learn to read, are being raised by an alcoholic parent, or have lost a parent in the war. Tell her you're proud of her and help her to find role models who have overcome the challenges she faces. And, be careful your child doesn't learn to use her disability as an excuse. For instance, "I can't behave. I have ADHD."

You can ask your local librarian to help you find books on the topic or research it on the Internet. You and your daughter can read about the role models together, discuss her feelings on the subject and identify strategies to help her live her life to its fullest.

Questions to Ponder

Think about your life and how it might impact your ability to help your children develop a strong sense of self.

- Are there things your parents could have done differently that might have been more helpful for you? For example, do you wish they had encouraged you to continue taking piano lessons or allowed you to quit dance class so you could have devoted more time to swimming?
- Could your parents have done more to help you pursue your interests and follow your dreams?
- How can you take what you learned from childhood and use it to be a better parent?
- Do you feel you've been able to follow your dreams or do you feel like something is still missing?
- Are you able to let your children pursue their own interests, or are there times when you catch yourself

wanting them to participate in particular activities more than they do?

If you think you might be trying to live your life through your children, step back and take a good look at your own life. Consider signing up for an activity yourself. Sure, you're probably too old to qualify for the Olympics or become a professional dancer, but you're not too old to take skiing lessons, go to law school, write a book, start acting, or learn how to play the piano.

By developing your own interests and pursuing your own goals, you will be better able to step back and allow your children to live their own lives in the ways that give them the most satisfaction.

After you look at your own life more closely, look at your children's lives.

- Do they seem happy?
- Are they becoming well adjusted and well rounded or are they spending their days and evenings glued to the TV or playing computer games?
- Do they enjoy interacting with others, learning new skills, and being creative or do they tend to isolate themselves from others and avoid opportunities to mature and develop?
- Are you helping your children learn to be more independent or are your fears preventing you from giving them opportunities to grow?
- Are you encouraging them to develop their own views and perspectives or are you insisting they see the world exactly as you see it?
- Are you comfortable letting them make their own mistakes or are you being too overprotective?

One of the best ways to find the answers to some of these questions is to sit down with your children and ask them. Talk with them about their values and discuss how you are similar to and different from them. Give your children opportunities to talk openly with you no matter how difficult the topic may be to discuss.

Most importantly, though, take the time to notice the unique people your children are becoming and tell them how proud you are to be their parent.

CHAPTER 3

SELF-CONFIDENCE

When we consider what it will take for our children to do well in life, we usually think of things like talent, skills, opportunities, and values. Those are all important, but sometimes we forget how important self-confidence can be.

What exactly is self-confidence? I'm sure you can recognize it when you see it, but how can you help your children develop it?

Self-confident people always possess one thing: a strong belief in themselves. They have faith that they'll be able to accomplish a goal even when others around them feel differently. If they fail, they don't give up. Instead of viewing themselves as failures, they see the situation as a challenge and look for new ways to accomplish their goals. Self-confident people know they can make things happen and feel that they deserve to do well in life.

People with strong self-confidence, even young children, carry themselves differently from those who lack this attribute. They make eye contact when they talk, present their opinions in a way that says "I know what I'm talking about and I believe my view is correct." They are willing to take risks and usually talk about themselves and their abilities in a positive way. Children with healthy self-confidence are the ones who are willing to demonstrate something in front of the class, be the first to try something new, or give a response that differs from those given by their peers. They don't stand on the sidelines waiting for opportunities to come their way. Instead, they often raise their hand and say "pick me," hoping to get an opportunity they feel they can handle and deserve.

Do children have to be born with good self-confidence? Of course not! Shy insecure kids can, and often do, grow up to be confident, outgoing adults, especially if they have a supportive adult in their lives.

Sometimes children possess a lot of self-confidence when they're younger but seem to lose it over time. For instance, a self-confident child may begin to feel more insecure when she moves from a small school where she was comfortable to a larger school where she feels lost. Many experiences can have a negative impact on a child's self-confidence such as divorce, teasing by peers, trauma or abuse, repeated failure, challenges such as learning disabilities or speech problems, and excessive criticism by parents, teachers, or coaches.

Some children are very self-confident in most aspects of their lives, while others are self-confident in some but not all situations. For example, you may have a child who is comfortable in social situations but lacks self-confidence in math class or one who feels at ease around adults, but is shy and withdrawn in an unstructured activity with peers.

Facts about Self-Confidence

Help your children improve their self-esteem by providing opportunities for them to experience success. Encourage your children to participate in activities in which they can feel competent and successful. They can participate in team sports, act in the school play, or serve as a volunteer to help younger kids learn to read.

When my children were in elementary school, they participated in a fourteen-week children's theater workshop that ended with them performing a play six times at a community theater. They learned skills, had a great time, and enjoyed all the applause they received each time they performed. This experience helped them feel comfortable performing in front of a large audience and also improved their self-confidence in school. After completing the workshop, they were more comfortable reading aloud, giving presentations and speeches, and expressing their opinions in class.

Help your children learn the skills they need to be successful. They aren't going to feel confident performing in a play if they don't know how to project their voices nor will they enjoy playing little league if they can't hit the ball. Take the time to teach your children the skills they need to become competent and confident. Being a good parent is time consuming, but we owe it to our kids to help them succeed in life. Spend time reading with your children every day. Help them with their homework. Teach them to tie their shoes, ride bikes, shoot baskets, and hit a baseball. Enroll them in activities where they can gain skills. They can take gymnastics classes, join the scouts, attend the Boys Club or Girls Club, or go to a camp at the Y, to name just a few of the opportunities available to kids today.

Help your children develop good personal hygiene habits. Teasing by peers can destroy a child's self-confidence and self-esteem. Ensure that your child is neat and clean when he goes to school each morning. Make sure that he has showered, washed and combed his hair, brushed his teeth, and is wearing clean clothes. Before he heads off to school in the morning, make sure his clothes fit him properly, and he doesn't look odd compared to his peers. In the past, low-income kids were at a real disadvantage. The most popular jeans were expensive and out of reach for some families, but now, thanks to used clothing stores, teens can purchase expensive jeans at bargain prices. They are used, but no one can tell the difference.

Help your children learn how to speak clearly. It's difficult for people to gain good self-confidence if they're uncomfortable speaking in front of people or in conversations. If your child has a speech impediment, seek help for her as soon as possible. The sooner she begins speech therapy, the better the prognosis.

My youngest daughter began to lose vocabulary at eighteen months. Her doctor suggested we have her evaluated and explained that the State Department of Health would cover the cost of the evaluation and the therapy. (If she were three years old or older, our local school system would have covered the costs.) Fortunately, when tubes were placed in her ears to treat her recurrent ear infections, she regained her speech and therapy wasn't needed. But it was comforting to know that services were available if she continued to have speech problems.

If your child has difficulty speaking, consult your doctor and school district and obtain the help your child needs. The longer a speech problem goes untreated, the more likely it will result in damage to your child's self-confidence.

As your children get older, help them to feel confident speaking in front of groups of people. Encourage them to be on the debate team, take a speech class, or audition for a part in the school play. Fortunately, today's teachers make public speaking a priority. Even in the lower grades, they require children to give presentations in front of the class or on stage in the auditorium. This gives them skills that many of us either developed when we were much older or, in some cases, failed to develop.

People who are self-confident accept their imperfections. We all have our faults, make mistakes, embarrass ourselves, and have limitations. People with a healthy self-confidence are able to acknowledge and accept these imperfections about themselves. Oprah Winfrey is a great example of this. She openly discusses things about herself that other people might hide out of a sense of shame or fear of being criticized or ridiculed. For example, she tells her audience when she gains weight and has shared many details about her past, including the fact that she was sexually abused as a child.

It's important to help your children become competent and feel that they deserve to be treated with respect. But how do you do that? Start by showing them that it's okay to like yourself despite your faults. Say things to them like, "I was never very good in softball, but that's okay. I was a great student. We all have our strengths and weaknesses" or "I tripped on my way into work and dropped everything. I had to laugh. Sometimes I can be such a klutz."

Talk to your children about how people are much less likely to tease them when they're open about their faults and able to laugh at themselves. Ask if they know any kids who are good at that and how their peers view them.

Discuss with your kids ways to improve their self-confidence. It's likely that your children have already given this a lot of thought. You may hear them say things like, "I wish I was thinner. I hate standing up in front of the class because I know I'm fatter than a lot of the other kids" or "I hate when the teacher asks me to read. I know I don't read very well."

Talk to your children about situations that make them feel uncomfortable or insecure and strategies they could use to gain self-confidence. For instance, suggest that the whole family eat less junk food and exercise more in order to maintain a healthy weight. Or ask an older sibling to teach his younger brother how to play baseball, or request an evaluation to determine if your child has a reading disability or might benefit from special education services.

Give your children opportunities to interact with older children. Did you ever notice that children who have older siblings are often more comfortable in social situations than an only child or those who don't have older siblings? Many activities group kids of several different ages together. This is a great way for them to develop confidence especially when they feel accepted by their older peers.

Present your children with opportunities to interact comfortably with adults. The days of children being seen but not heard are over. Today many adults ask children to call them by their first name and occasionally include them in discussions. Children who are invited to participate in conversations with adults (about appropriate topics, of course) develop self-confidence. For example, if your child is with you when you're talking to adults about who should be president, ask her which candidate she would vote for if she were old enough to vote. When your friends visit, ask your child to tell them about her scouting trip, swimming lessons, new puppy, or dance recital.

Provide opportunities for your children to feel comfortable in different environments and with different people. There are so many ways you can expose your children to different environments and people. At my job, parents bring their school-age children to Take Your Son/Daughter to Work Day. This is a great way for kids to begin to feel comfortable in a work environment. Many college students study or do volunteer work in other countries. It offers them opportunities to experience different cultures, live in different countries, eat different foods, interact with people from different socio-economic groups, and sometimes even speak different languages. These experiences are attainable for students from low-income or high-income families alike and can have a profound impact on their lives.

Help your children develop social skills. It's hard to have self-confidence when you're socially awkward. Some children pick up social skills naturally, while others struggle to develop these skills. Encourage your children to make eye contact when they speak, to sit and stand up straight, and to not monopolize conversations or interrupt people when they are speaking. Teach them manners and to show respect for others. If your child is struggling with these skills, ask if a social worker or counselor provides social skills groups for the students at his school. You can also contact therapists who treat children or your local mental health clinic to see if there are any social skills groups available in your community.

Children feel more self-confident when they have the necessary skills to have their needs met. People who wait for others to identify and meet their needs are often disappointed, while those who are more assertive are

more likely to get what they want. It can be difficult to
teach your children how to be assertive if you've never
learned these skills or don't understand the difference
between assertiveness and aggression. When people are
assertive, they are aware of the needs of the other person. Unlike an aggressive person, an assertive person
verbalizes needs in a respectful way that does not hurt
the other person or impinge on his or her rights. For
example, when a child cuts in line, an aggressive child
might push the child out of the way and call her a nasty
name. An assertive child is more likely to look the other
child in the eye and say, "I've been standing here. You
need to stand behind me" in a confident tone of voice,
and then move in front of the other child.

If your child has difficulty being assertive, practice
these skills at home by role-playing various situations
she may encounter at school. Ask her teacher to help her
develop these skills by supporting her when she at-
tempts to be assertive and praising her for expressing
her opinions clearly and respectfully.

*Self-confident people believe they have a right to
express their own opinions, even when others disagree
with them.* We all want our children to behave, listen to
us, and follow our directions, but we need to be careful
we don't raise overly compliant children who are afraid
to speak their minds. Especially as your children get
older, it's important to let them disagree with you sometimes (and they will). Watch the news with your child
and talk with him about controversial issues. Encourage
him to present strong arguments to support his views
and let him know it's okay for the two of you to see
things differently.

Empower your children. When your child is mistreated, encourage her to stand up for herself and not let
other people walk all over her. When she identifies a

goal, empower her to reach it. For example, if she really wants to take an accelerated class, encourage her to e-mail her teacher or ask to speak with him after class. Talk to her about how she could argue for an opportunity to be placed in the more advanced class. If your son wants to start a fund-raising project, discuss ways he could raise money and let him know that you'll back him one hundred percent.

Provide opportunities for your child to develop leadership skills. Today kids have so many more opportunities to gain leadership skills than we had. Ask your children's teachers or guidance counselors what opportunities are available at their school or in your community. Encourage your children to hold offices in student government, 4-H clubs, or in a scout troop. Ask how teens can chair community service committees, organize fund-raising events and educational activities, and attend leadership training programs. If you look on the Internet, you will find many leadership camps your kids could attend, some of which offer full scholarships. Encourage your children to participate in these programs and talk with them about how important these skills will be in helping them reach their goals in life.

Praise your children and remind them you're proud of them even when they did their best but failed. Don't assume that your kids know when they did a good job. Tell them and be specific when you provide praise so they will know what they did right. For example, if your child did a great job in the school play you might say, "You were wonderful. You remembered all of your lines, you looked out at the audience, and you spoke loudly. People really enjoyed your performance." Remind them that you admire their hard work as much as their success. You might say, "I know you didn't win the spelling bee, but I'm so proud of you. You worked really hard these past few weeks." Praise your children but try to avoid paying them for success. Some research has shown that tangible rewards may, at least temporarily, diminish the intrinsic reward of doing a good job and accomplishing a goal and may actually reduce their motivation to succeed in the future.

In situations where you need to help your child over a tough hurdle to get him started on a difficult path, you might consider rewarding him with a preferred activity or tangible item AFTER he takes the initial steps. Then begin to replace the activity or item with praise.

Be careful not to be too critical. Constructive feedback is helpful to kids, but we all know that criticism, if presented in an angry way, can damage our self-confidence. Never make demeaning remarks to your kids or call them nasty names. That's a line you should never cross. For example, never say something like, "You looked like an idiot up there. You didn't even know your lines." Instead consider saying, "This wasn't your best performance. I think you might have done better if you had spent more time practicing your lines instead of playing your video games so much. What do you think?"

Start building your child's self-confidence right from the start. Even when your children are very young, it is important for you to start building their self-confidence. They need to grow up hearing things like, "I knew you'd learn how to do it," "Great job," "You are so smart," and "Go ahead. Give it a try. I bet you can do it."

Never encourage your children to cheat, lie about their performance, or exaggerate when you talk about their accomplishments. Sometimes parents do these things in an effort to help their children reach their goals, but that sort of behavior is extremely damaging to a child and undermines their ability to succeed in life.

For example, if you tell someone that your child earned straight A's when he earned 2 A's and 3 B's, what you are really saying is, "I have to lie and say that his grades were higher than they were because I'm embarrassed to admit he didn't get all A's." The message to the child is he's a failure and an embarrassment to you. The same holds true for cheating. If you encourage your child to cheat, you are telling her that she doesn't have the ability to win honestly. Again, the message is that she is a failure. If you are doing these things, ask yourself why it is so important for your child to succeed. Are you doing it for your child or are you doing it for yourself?

Don't let your anxiety undermine your child's confidence. Most of us feel a little anxious when our children try to learn a new skill such as riding a bike or skiing, take a risk such as performing on stage for the first time, or enter a competition such as a spelling bee or gymnastics meet. But some parents become so nervous they undermine their children's ability to feel confident. If you are one of those parents, you need to learn to control your emotions. Keep quiet, step back, and let your child participate in the activity without interfering.

If your fear of your child falling is going to prevent him from learning to ride a bike, ask someone else to teach him. If you're going to bombard your daughter with advice prior to a tennis match, ask someone else to drive her to the match, watch her from a distance, and don't talk to her until the game is over. If you feel that, because of your anxiety, you're preventing your child from taking risks that will help her grow and become more confident, consider talking to a therapist. Chances are good that your issues are interfering with your ability to be a good parent.

Take action if your child is assigned to a bad teacher.
Nothing can damage a child's self-confidence as a student more than ridicule from a teacher. Most teachers are fantastic, but occasionally a student has a teacher who chose the wrong occupation. You'll know if that's the case with your child. He'll begin to hate school, will come up with excuses to stay home, and probably say derogatory things about himself as a student. If that happens to your child, meet with his teacher immediately. Notice how she talks about him. Does she say positive things or is she too critical? Ask if you can observe your child in class, consider meeting with the principal, and talk with other parents who have children in your child's class. If necessary, insist that your child be given another teacher.

Ensure that relatives support your efforts to help your children develop self-confidence. Children don't grow up to be self-confident if others repeatedly demean or insult them. As parents we're responsible for protecting our children from harm, including emotional abuse by relatives. Don't allow anyone, even your parents or siblings, to insult your children, call them names, or favor one over another. If that happens, make it clear you won't tolerate that behavior. You can say, "If you are going to give one child a gift, you need to give something to all of the children so that none of them feels left out." You might also say something like, "I told you several times not to tell Josh he's stupid. If you continue to do that, I am going to stop inviting you over for dinner. Those comments hurt his feelings, and I won't allow you to come into my house and say hurtful things to my children."

Protect your children from ridicule by peers and siblings. In the past, people thought that fighting among siblings was a normal part of growing up. It's true that siblings will fight and do need to have opportunities to learn to resolve conflicts on their own, but ongoing physical or emotional cruelty from siblings can be very damaging and should never be tolerated. As a parent, it's your responsibility to stop it. You may need to take family members to a therapist or consider enrolling in a parenting class.

Ongoing ridicule from peers is also damaging. If your child is being picked on by kids at school or in the neighborhood, encourage her to stand up for herself. If that doesn't work, intervene and put a stop to it. Meet with your child's teacher or guidance counselor or call the parents of the children who are teasing her. Let them know how your child is being affected by the teasing and ask for their help in solving the problem. Let your child know she deserves to be treated with respect and show her that you will intervene in order to protect her.

Questions to Ponder

Were you self-confident as a child? If so, what helped you become that way? If not, how could your parents have helped you to develop more self-confidence?

- How about now? Have you become more self-confident as you've grown older or do you wish you could feel better about yourself and your abilities? If you lack self-confidence, what could you do to improve it?
- Are your children self-confident? Are there some areas where they're more self-confident than others or is one of your children more or less self-confident than your other children?
- What do you think is responsible for the differences?
- Do you talk to your children about how they feel about themselves?
- Do you know what situations make them anxious

and which ones make them feel most confident?

- Do you give them opportunities to take risks and develop new skills or are you too overprotective because of your own anxiety?
- Have you shared with your children your own experiences while growing up?
- Have you talked with them about how you felt in various situations and how your feelings about yourself changed as you got older?
- Do you protect your children from ridicule or emotional abuse?
- Do you help them develop skills they'll need to feel confident with their peers, when interacting with adults, when speaking to others and when giving presentations in front of groups of people?

CHAPTER 4

COPING WITH STRESS

When we think about childhood, we usually picture kids running and playing on the playground, laughing with friends, or riding their bikes. Childhood has the reputation for being a carefree time when kids can have fun and grow before becoming adults. We strive to make those early years as stress free as possible for our children and hope to create happy memories that will stay with them for a lifetime.

Despite our best efforts, however, for many kids childhood is far from free of stress. Years ago, life was slower and children enjoyed more quiet time. When we were growing up, school placed fewer demands on students, and we had much more free unstructured time than kids today have. When we participated in activities such as sports and clubs, the commitment was minimal. Today some activities, such as gymnastics and competitive dance, require children to attend practices for two or three hours a day, six days a week in addition to participating in competitions and fund-raising events. We shuffle our kids from one activity to another, encourage them to do well in school, and then wonder why they're so stressed out. We don't want to deny our children opportunities to be successful in the activities they love, but we struggle to keep things in perspective.

Even school has made life much more stressful for kids. Today when teenagers take advanced placement courses, they usually have to study several hours a night for each course. When my oldest daughter took her first advanced placement course, I was surprised to learn that she would have to begin completing assignments a month before the start of the school year and would be expected to complete several hours of work each day on holidays and during vacations. The stress of taking these advanced courses combines with the pressure kids feel about getting into a good college. They take SAT preparation courses, worry about their class rank, and pack their already full schedules with numerous extracurricular and volunteer activities, knowing that competitive colleges won't even consider them unless they are well-rounded, active members of their school and community.

The pressure in school starts early. My children attend a small school in a rural community. It isn't a private school and few of the children in the district apply to top colleges. It doesn't have the competitive environment found in many larger schools or in more affluent areas, but the pressure is still there. When we took our children to Florida during a school vacation years ago, I was surprised when my oldest daughter's teacher assigned a great deal of reading and math for the children to complete during vacation. Rachel was only seven or eight at the time, and I had hoped that the vacation would give her a break from school. I thought she would be able to enjoy time with the family, relax and escape from the pressures of school for a week, but I was wrong.

Schools want children to succeed, but I think it's also important for them to have breaks from the pressure of school and opportunities to relax and play. We already have enough workaholics in the world and don't need to create a new generation of them. Don't get me wrong! I believe that learning academic skills such as reading and math is very important for children, but they also need to learn how to relax, play, socialize with peers, and develop other aspects of their personalities. After all, we don't just want our children to be smart and successful. We also want them to enjoy life to its fullest, maintain a healthy lifestyle so they live for a long time and develop meaningful, healthy relationships.

We know stress can be dangerous. It can reduce the quality of life, as well as a person's life expectancy and cause people to develop serious health problems such as high blood pressure and cardiovascular problems.

So how do we help our children cope effectively with the stressors in their lives?

Facts about Coping with Stress

Stress isn't always a bad thing. It drives us to make changes in our lives and motivates us to take action. A child who is experiencing the stress of boredom may get off the couch and find a book to read or go outside to play. A child who is anxious about an upcoming test may study a little harder, and one who is feeling stressed out about participating in so many after school activities may decide to drop one or two activities in order to make his life more manageable. Stressors by themselves are not bad. They become negative when they are too severe or chronic or the person is trying to cope with too many stressors at once and lacks the ability to cope effectively with them.

Positive events can be stressful, too. When we think of stressors, we usually think of negative things like illnesses or fear of failure, but positive events can be just as stressful. For example, a young child may feel overwhelmed by the excitement of a birthday party, or her father returning from the war, or the excitement of leaving for a family vacation.

If your child becomes overwhelmed easily, keep positive events simple. You could invite a smaller number of friends to her birthday party, have a quiet family reunion with her father rather than a large party, or avoid talking about the vacation until a day or two before you leave for your trip. Try to keep her routine in place as much as possible and ensure that she gets enough rest.

Children's responses to stress vary greatly. No two children respond to stress in the same way. As parents, we learn over time how each of our children responds to stress. They may become irritable, angry, have difficulty sleeping, or become anxious or withdrawn. Some children will get stomach aches, headaches, or say that they feel sick, while others will have more difficulty tolerating changes in routine or seem depressed. The important thing is to watch your children for signs that they are experiencing too much stress. Talk with them about the situation, ask them how you can make things better for them, suggest ways they can cope, and reduce stress in their lives as much as possible.

Children need to learn how to self-soothe. One of the most important things we teach our children is how to self-soothe. In other words, how to comfort themselves and cope effectively with the intense emotions that stressors produce. But how do you teach your child to do this? Self-soothing is something you start teaching your child right from the beginning. You want to do whatever you can to make your baby feel safe and secure. When he cries, pick him up and let him know you are there for him. Comfort him by rocking him, singing lullabies to him, and holding him close to you. Give him a favorite blanket or stuffed animal to hold when you put him to bed and encourage him to hold it when he's in situations that may be stressful for him such as his first day at day care, a doctor's appointment, or the day his new sibling comes home from the hospital. When he's upset, pick him up and reassure him he'll be okay.

Model appropriate ways to handle stress. We all know that children do what we do, not what we say. Chances are good your children will grow up to cope with stress in the same ways you cope with it. If you take your stress out on other people, it's likely your children will do the same. Therefore, it's especially important when you're stressed you don't let your children see you take your stress out on others. No matter how stressed you are, avoid yelling at your family, throwing things, harming the pets, or being rude to your spouse or kids. Those are lines you just can't cross as a parent. It's also important you don't use alcohol or drugs to cope. Don't come home from a tough day at work and say, "I am so stressed out, I need to pour myself a drink" and then spend the evening drinking. The same is true of drugs, including prescription drugs designed to reduce anxiety.

Instead, model more appropriate methods for reducing stress. Go for a walk, take a bath, have a cup of coffee, watch a movie, play a game with the kids, or read a good book. Explain to your child that you're extremely stressed and have found these things help you relax and feel better. Ask your child what makes her feel better when she's stressed.

If your child is finding school stressful, talk to her teacher or guidance counselor. I've found that teachers are very responsive when they learn that children in their class are feeling stressed or anxious over their schoolwork. Today, all teachers have e-mail and appreciate it when a parent sends a quick note about a problem their child is having. I let teachers know if my kids are struggling with homework or feel they haven't mastered a concept being taught. Teachers will set up times during or after school to provide additional help or will ask the class if they are having similar problems. It's not uncommon for teachers to give their class a day off from homework when they learn their students are feeling stressed.

Avoid burdening your kids with unnecessary stress. As parents, we often feel stressed. If you're feeling that way, it's important to cope with your feelings and not burden your children with them. They have enough to deal with and we need to remember they are the children, and we are the parents. It's our job to take care of them, not visa versa.

If you've lost your job, don't share with your child the worry about possibly losing your house, too. No child needs to worry about becoming homeless. If your job is at risk, it's okay to tell your teen or older child you're nervous about your job if they ask, but leave them with a feeling of hope. You could say, "They are laying off a lot of people at work and I do worry, but I'm a good worker and I'm sure they'll keep me if they can" or "I don't want to lose my job, but if I do I'm sure I'll find another one. I always have in the past."

If you feel you need to talk to someone about your stress, find an adult to help you. Talk to your spouse or close friend. Consider going to therapy or finding a support group. Many people who are unemployed have formed groups that meet at local restaurants and coffee shops. They serve as support groups, as well as provide opportunities for networking.

Find ways to make your home life less stressful. Most of us live stressful, hectic lives. Help your children by reducing stress in the home as much as possible. Consider identifying times when you won't talk on the phone, watch TV, or answer e-mails. Reduce noise whenever possible by turning off the TV when no one is watching it. If you can afford it, consider paying someone to clean your house, mow the lawn, or do the gardening. I find that my life is a lot calmer when my home is more organized. If everything seems be out of control in your house, ask everyone in the family to pitch in. Straighten up messy closets, organize papers and books, throw out junk mail, write appointments on a calendar, and take care of those errands you've been avoiding.

Plan ahead. Don't wait until the last minute to accomplish tasks. Mornings are stressful in most households, but you can make things run much smoother if you plan ahead. Have your daughter pick out her clothes the night before school so she won't have a melt down in the morning when she learns her favorite pink sweater is in the wash. Five minutes before the bus comes is not the time to find matching socks, lost homework, or gym clothes.

Make stress reduction a priority. Try to find ways that you and your family can reduce stress and rejuvenate yourselves. When my kids were little, we used to take mini-vacations in the winter. We'd spend one night in a local hotel with a pool and hot tub. By staying near home, my husband could run home and let the dogs out, and we wouldn't have the added stress, expense, and pressure of having to take them to a kennel. The hotel didn't cost much and an evening of swimming, relaxing in the hot tub, eating out, and watching movies in the room was a great way for us to relax and have fun as a family. If taking a mini vacation isn't possible, consider having a picnic at a local park, taking the kids to a playground, or scheduling a weekly family activity such as movie or game night.

Set boundaries and learn to say no. The truth is you can't do it all. None of us are superheroes. Don't be afraid to say "No." If you're coping with a serious illness, studying for exams at college, taking care of a newborn, or working long hours during a busy time at work, you may have reached your limits and not have the energy to entertain relatives over the holidays or coordinate special events at your child's school. We all have our limits and if you feel you can't cope with any more stress or take on any more responsibility, don't be afraid to say "no." Explain that, although you would love to help out, you really can't help right now but you'd be glad to help at another time when you don't have so much on your plate. Most people will understand. (Don't worry about those who don't.)

Help your children stay healthy. It's difficult for any of us to cope with stress when we're sick, stressed, or tired, and our children are no different. Ensure that your children get enough sleep every night, especially when they're under a lot of pressure. Serve nutritious meals and provide them with plenty of opportunities to get exercise and fresh air. Don't let them skip meals or fill up on junk food.

Provide opportunities for your children to have fun. People have difficulty coping with stressors when they are depressed or unhappy. Play with your kids and provide opportunities for them to play with their friends. Riding bikes or shooting baskets with friends can do wonders to help a frazzled kid relax. If you have pets, you've probably noticed an improvement in your child's mood after she's spent some time petting the cat or taking the dog for a walk. Some kids enjoy taking care of plants, building model cars, drawing, or singing, while others relax by writing poems, playing with their dolls, or watching movies.

Consider seeking professional help for your child. If your child seems to be too stressed, consider taking him to a therapist. Explain you are concerned about him and believe he'll feel better if he talks to a professional. Let him know that seeking help at times of need is a good thing and nothing of which to be ashamed.

Be supportive and compassionate. Talk to your child about her stress. Listen as she tells you how she feels and provide validation. For example, say, "It sounds like you're under a lot of pressure at school, and I agree that the workload is too much." Don't be too rigid with rules. You might say, "I know I said you need to do the dishes every night, but you have too much homework tonight. I'll be glad to do them for you until things calm down."

Problem solve with your child. As your children grow older, they are going to face many stressful situations in life and will have to learn how to cope with them on their own. You can't go to college with your son or help him cope with pressure at work when he's out there on his own. What you can do, though, is to help him develop coping skills. Talk with him about ways he can handle stress. Ask him which things he can change and which ones he can't. Suggest ways he can reduce stress like exercising or spending time with friends, and remind him that alcohol and drugs are never the answer. Encourage him to talk with teachers if his school-work is becoming too difficult or consider quitting an after school job if the stress of working while going to school becomes more than he can handle. Help him to understand that sometimes you have to say no to people or make changes in your life in order to make your life manageable.

Take care of yourself. Your children are going to feel anxious when you're stressed, no matter how hard you try to prevent that from happening. Reduce your own stress by taking care of yourself. Spend time with friends, go out for a romantic dinner with your spouse, exercise, eat properly, and participate in enjoyable activities. Take a look at yourself. How well are you managing your stress? Are you meeting the needs of your family but neglecting your own? Are you coping well or do you need more support?

Questions to Ponder

Think back to your childhood.

- How did your parents cope with stress when you were growing up? Did they drink heavily, yell a lot, or withdraw from the family?
- When was life most stressful in your house when you were growing up? Was it when your father lost his job, a new baby was born, when your family was having financial problems, or maybe when your parents' marriage was in trouble?
- How did you feel when your parents were stressed?
- How did they respond to you during those times? Did they talk with you and ask you how you felt or were they too consumed with their own problems to help you?
- Did you have an adult in your life who provided support and reassured you that you'd be okay?

- Are there things you wish your parents had done differently that might have made your life less stressful when you were growing up?
- What situations make your children feel most stressed?
- Do you talk with them about their feelings?
- Do you model good coping strategies and teach them effective ways to cope?
- Do you talk with their teachers when they're feeling stressed at school?
- Do you help your children identify ways to make their lives less stressful?
- Do you ensure their lives are filled with opportunities to have fun and that they have relationships with compassionate and supportive adults?

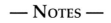

— NOTES —

CHAPTER 5

COPING WITH CRISES

We'd all like our children to travel through child-hood without hitting too many bumps along the way. Unfortunately, though, the road is not a smooth one for many kids. Some experience physical, sexual, or emo-tional abuse. Others develop a serious illness such as cancer or chronic medical conditions like diabetes or asthma. There are children who grow up in high crime neighborhoods where they become witnesses to and victims of violence and others who must cope with poverty. Some children are injured in car accidents or experience trauma as the result of a flood, fire, or home invasion. Many children are negatively affected by the experience of undergoing a painful medical procedure.

Childhood years are usually thought of as the care-free years. We picture children playing on the swings at school or riding bikes around the neighborhood with friends, but for many kids those years can be traumatic. Bullying by peers can cause children to become so depressed they take their own lives or leave them with scars that last a lifetime.

Children don't have to actually experience negative events in order to be harmed. Growing up in a home with domestic violence can severely traumatize a child, as can witnessing a violent crime, severe car accident, or a death.

Sounds hopeless, doesn't it? Well, don't despair. Children are very resilient. With help and support, they can not only survive traumatic events but they can develop skills to cope effectively with future stressors. We've all heard stories of people who endured great hardships in childhood and went on to accomplish amazing feats as adults. Bill Clinton went from being the child of an alcoholic father to becoming President of the United States. As mentioned, Oprah Winfrey was poor and the victim of sexual abuse as a child but now is one of the most successful and influential people in our country.

So how do we not only help our children survive crises but actually use those experiences to become stronger, more resilient adults?

Facts about Coping with Crises

Everyone will have to cope with crises in his or her lifetime. When children face a crisis, they invariably feel as if they're the only person who has to deal with such a thing. Most ask, "Why me?" and wonder what they did to cause such a terrible thing to happen. It's important to help them understand that no one can go through life without having to cope with crises or experiencing traumas. Everyone will have friends and family members die, develop some type of health problem if they live long enough, and hit various other bumps in the road. They may not have to cope with a terminal illness or significant loss in childhood, but they will invariably experience traumatic events of some sort.

My daughter was upset when we discovered she has a cardiac condition. I explained to her it's true most kids don't have this medical problem but that a lot of kids struggle with something. Some of her classmates live in poverty. Others have learning disabilities or suffer from asthma or diabetes. Several children in her school have lost a mother and many, if not the majority, have divorced parents. One of her best friends lost everything in a house fire, and a local flood left many families temporarily homeless.

As my daughter has grown older, she's come to understand that she's not alone. She tells me that, although she used to think her medical condition was horrible, she now realizes it has very little impact on the quality of her life. "It really doesn't affect me much," she tells me. She knows her health is much better than doctors initially anticipated and that most people can't tell there is anything different about her.

Help your child connect with other children who are coping with similar crises. Contact a local hospital or human service agency and find out if there are any support groups available for children coping with similar stressors. Most community hospitals have support groups for kids coping with cancer, diabetes, asthma, and death of a loved one. Schools provide support for children coping with a natural disaster or death of a classmate. To find out what is available, contact your child's guidance counselor or look on the school web site.

The Internet is a great way for many kids to find support from their peers. Most national organizations provide Internet chat rooms for older children and teens and offer activities for them at regional and national conferences.

Help your child realize that an end to their discomfort or present plight is in sight. We know people can cope more effectively when they know that eventually their struggle will end. Medical professionals are very good at this. If your child is undergoing a painful medical procedure, you'll hear the doctors and nurses say things like, "This is going to be painful, but it will last for only about sixty seconds. I'm going to begin," and then "we're half way through, just thirty seconds more. You are doing great."

The same applies to other stressors and crises. If your house is flooded, let your child know it's being remodeled, and you'll be back home in a month or so. If he loses a friend, explain to him that he'll feel terribly sad for a while, but over time things will get better. Remind him of the fun he had riding bikes and fishing with his friend and explain that no one can ever take those memories away from him.

When your child says that she's angry, validate her feelings. If your child is coping with a crisis, it's perfectly normal for her to feel angry. For instance, if her sister dies, she's likely to feel both sad and angry. That's perfectly normal. Validate her feelings. You might say, "I'm angry, too, that she died. I loved her so much, and I know it's not her fault that she died, but I'm still really mad she's gone." Explain that bad feelings are okay, but that she needs to talk about them and not act them out. You could say, "You can be mad and yell sometimes, but it's not okay to hit your brother or break his things."

Jealousy is a normal reaction to stressors and trauma, too. We all feel jealous at times, and kids are no exception. Help your child understand that it's okay to feel jealous, but help him understand it's important not to let his jealousy destroy his relationships. For example, you could say, "I know sometimes you're jealous because Joshua's dad attends all his games and your dad doesn't. It's all right to be jealous, but don't let your feelings ruin your friendship with Joshua. If you stop hanging out with him, I think you'll really miss him."

Children dealing with crises usually regress. If your child experiences a crisis, you're likely to see her exhibit behaviors or respond in ways more typical of younger children. For example, your elementary school child may wet the bed again after being the victim of a home invasion, your toddler may become more clingy and afraid to let you out of her sight, and your teen may start sleeping with her stuffed animals again or whine as she did when she was younger. Don't worry if that happens. Listen to the message your child is sending you, and provide her with the additional support she needs. If her problems continue for more than a few weeks, consider having her see a therapist.

Help your child mourn losses. When we think of loss, we think of things like the death of a loved one or a friend moving away. Sometimes we don't realize that other experiences can be losses, too, such as losing the ability to participate in a favorite sport because of serious sports injury, having to give up the dream of becoming a professional dancer after developing scoliosis, or losing the innocence of childhood after being molested by a teacher or religious leader.

When children experience loss, they need to have the opportunity to grieve. Ask your son how he feels about the loss and then sit quietly and listen. Let him know you're listening and care about how he feels. Tell him it's okay to cry and that you feel sad, too. Be careful not to disclaim the validity of his feelings. Refrain from saying things like, "It was just a hamster" or "There's more to life than playing basketball."

Give your child opportunities to help. Helping others is one of the best ways to help yourself in a time of crisis. The same is true for our children. Even young children can help others. Your child with cancer can give a toy to the kid in the next bed, your teen who lost everything in a flood can volunteer to distribute clothing to other flood victims, and your child who lost a grandparent can continue to visit other elderly patients at the nursing home where his grandmother lived.

I had open-heart surgery when my oldest daughter was just four years old. The nursing staff did a great job allowing her to help me. They let her get me sodas from the refrigerator whenever I was thirsty and push my IV pole when I went for short walks on the unit. They praised Rachel for being such a good helper and reminded her she played an important role in my recovery.

Keep your child's teacher informed about the problems your child is facing. Teachers tend to be incredibly supportive of children coping with severe stressors. They'll excuse them from homework, give them extensions on due dates for papers, and cut them a break when they're talking during class or having difficulty staying focused.

When my youngest daughter was in kindergarten, my husband became very sick with what was later diagnosed as Lyme disease. One day, Megan was upset because she knew her father was going to have some medical tests at a hospital an hour or so away. She was scared the doctors might do something to hurt him, like give him a shot. I spoke to her teacher that morning and explained what was happening. Her teacher gave Megan extra attention and even let her sit on her lap most of the day.

Give your child opportunities to feel in control and to make choices. Crises often take away a person's sense of control. It is so important to help your child have control over at least some aspects of her life. Find things you are willing to let her control and offer her choices. You could let her decide what the family will eat for dinner or plan a family activity for the weekend.

Provide opportunities for your child to have fun. Play can be extremely healing for children. It's common, for example, for a child to want to attend the birthday party of a friend just days after the death of a parent or to ask to take a friend to the movies despite coping with a parent leaving the home. Although these things may seem odd to an adult, they can be a healing force for a child.

Be careful what you discuss within hearing distance of your children. It's not uncommon for children to eavesdrop on adult conversations, but they are likely to do this even more frequently when they sense that their parents are stressed. Be careful not to discuss things that may traumatize or frighten your children. For example, if you and your spouse need to talk about your fears that your child may die from his cancer, hire a sitter and go some place away from home to have that discussion or consider addressing these issues in therapy.

Don't provide more information than your child is asking for. Children know how much information they can handle, and they don't want you to tell them about all the horrible things that could potentially happen to them. For example, if your child wants to know how many chemotherapy treatments he needs, that's what you should tell him. Avoid providing information about the likelihood the chemo may not work or the odds that he'll survive unless the additional information is positive and will assist in reducing his stress.

Help your child to feel secure. Crises will cause your child to feel scared and insecure. Remind her often that you love her and will do everything in your power to keep her safe. It's okay to let your elementary school child sleep in bed with you for a few nights or keep the light on in her room if it makes her feel safer and more secure.

Educate your child with information at a level he can comprehend. Avoid the use of big words or fancy terms. Ask your child to tell you how she understands the situation. Find books or information on the Internet that will help her better understand what's happening to her. Ask your librarian if books are available that address a particular topic at a level your child will understand.

Always give your child a sense of hope. Some people become very negative when feeling depressed. If you are one of those people, be careful not to pass that on to your child. Avoid making remarks like, "I don't think we'll ever get this mess cleaned up and be able to move back home" or "I'll never get a job. We're going to lose the house. I just know we will." Instead say things like, "Things are tough right now, but they'll get better soon" or "You are a survivor. You're going to get through this. I know you will."

Help your child express herself. Children have a difficult time putting feelings into words. Young children often express themselves through play or art, or they act out their feelings through behaviors. An angry or sad child may throw a tantrum. A frightened child may become clingy or withdrawn.

Older children and teens may engage in puzzling or worrisome behavior and have difficulty talking about their feelings. Some young people express their feelings more easily through creative writing, journaling, or art.

A good way to get kids to open up is by going on a long ride in the car. That allows you and your child to talk, but you don't have to make eye contact. Your child can look out the window while slowly opening up about how she feels.

Watch for signs of post-traumatic stress disorder, depression, or anxiety. Children who have been traumatized often have nightmares, excessive fear and anxiety, difficulty concentrating, and increased startle responses. They may withdraw and have recurrent thoughts about the traumatic event. You may notice increased anxiety, including panic attacks or signs of depression, like sadness, loss of interest in activities, and even suicidal thoughts. They may sleep too much, wake up throughout the night, or have trouble falling asleep. Some children have excessive weight gain or weight loss, cry often, or report feeling depressed.

Take your child to a mental health provider if you think the crisis or trauma is negatively impacting his mental health. Ask him if he has any concerns or would like help coping with his current situation. Seek professional help immediately if he is talking about suicide or his peers are worried he may kill himself. You can call 911 or the mental health crisis center at your local hospital.

Try to reduce your child's stress until the crisis is over. If your child must undergo medical treatment for a serious health problem, deal with a loss, or cope with trauma, suggest he reduce the stress in his life until the crisis is over. Try not to give him additional responsibilities at home and suggest he take an easier course load at school. Consider downsizing holiday celebrations, schedule fewer activities, and spend more time together as a family until life begins to return to normal.

Remind your child that the crisis is not his fault.
Most of the time, your child is not responsible for the
crisis she is facing. It's not her fault' she developed
health problems, your marriage fell apart, or the house
flooded, yet she may feel it is. Younger children, in
particular, often blame themselves for things that are
clearly out of their control. Talk with your child and ask
her if she feels responsible for what happened. Explain
that it's not her fault.

Sometimes kids are at fault. Your son may have
started the fire in the house when he hid a lit cigarette
under his bed. Your daughter may have played a role in
the dog's death when she chose to let the dog run loose
so she wouldn't have to walk him in the rain. In those
cases, you need to help your child understand that
everyone makes mistakes. Stress it is important for
them to take responsibility for their actions and then
learn from their mistakes. Tell them you forgive them
and hope they'll forgive themselves. If necessary, take
your child to therapy to work through his or her guilt.

Avoid being overprotective. Your children will face
crises as they are growing up. You need to protect them,
but don't be so overprotective that you deny them
opportunities to take reasonable risks, make mistakes,
and grow from these experiences. We all made mistakes
when we were growing up and your children will, too.
Try not to be too hard on them. Childhood should be a
time of adventure and fun. Try to view small crises as
opportunities for your children to learn how to cope
effectively with stressors and to develop the skills and
resilience they'll need in life.

Questions to Ponder

Think about the challenges you've faced in life as a child and now as an adult.

- Have loved ones died?
- Have you had to cope with illness or tragedy?

Consider your own childhood.

- What events or circumstances were most stressful for you?
- How well did you cope with them, and who was most supportive of you?
- Did you become more resilient as a result of coping with the crisis or do you feel you were emotionally scarred by the experience?
- How do you help your children cope with crises? Are you able to help them talk about their feelings and comfort them?
- Do you help them feel safe and secure or does your own stress and anxiety make it difficult for you to do so?
- What are some ways you can help your family reduce stress during times of crisis?

— NOTES —

CHAPTER 6

KINDNESS

Parents often disagree about who they hope their children will become. Some dream of them attending prestigious universities and going on to become award-winning scientists, writers, or researchers. Others picture their kids playing professional sports, performing on Broadway, or breaking world records. Some parents encourage their children to devote their lives to helping others, improving the environment, or raising a family.

One thing most parents have in common, though, is a desire for their children to grow up to become good people. When we go to parent-teacher conferences, we hope the teacher will say things like, "Kate is such a great kid. I really enjoy having her in my class;" "Andrew is so kind. He always sticks up for the underdog." "Evan has so many friends. Everyone in the class loves him."

Most of us want our children to grow up to be respectable, caring and compassionate adults. We hope we'll enjoy spending time with them when they're grown, and that they'll be there for us when we're old. Unfortunately, though, not all children become good adults. Our prison system is full of people who victimize others for their own personal gain, and we have all crossed paths with people who are nasty and dishonest.

So how do we make sure our children grow up to be kind, respectable people?

Facts about Kindness

Although everyone probably would say they want their children to become nice people, some parents convey a very different message to their children. If you tell your child it's okay to cheat or to victimize others in order to get what they want out of life, you're giving him the message that winning is more important than being a good person. This may help him reach his goals in the short term but is unlikely to help him grow up to have a happy and successful life.

Today, networking is more important than ever to career success. Nasty, self-serving people often find that co-workers are unlikely to recommend them for jobs and promotions. Although they may move to the front of the pack initially, as years go by they often experience failure in their careers and struggle to understand how that could have happened.

Bernie Madoff was one of those who looked highly successful even though he was dishonest and gained his wealth by victimizing others. He may have gained more wealth than most of us could ever imagine having, but it's not doing him much good now as he sits in prison. Instill in your children the importance of achieving success through hard work and honesty and the knowledge that success alone does not lead to happiness.

Think about the example you set for your children. Do they see you helping others, or are you always placing your own needs first? Do they see you holding the door for others or pushing your way to the front of the line? Do they overhear you talking to your spouse about the importance of being honest when selling your old car, or do they witness you trying to rip off an unsuspecting buyer?

It is important to bond with your children. Spend time alone with your child holding, cuddling, kissing, and talking to him. When he's a newborn, look into his eyes and allow yourself to fall in love with him.

Some parents have difficulty bonding with their babies, especially if they didn't have a healthy attachment to their own parents. If this is the case for you, give yourself plenty of quiet time alone with your baby. Consider asking family members to visit at a later time so you and your spouse can bond with the baby. Tell them you think this is important for you and your child and that you appreciate their support and cooperation. Remind them that you'll be glad to give them time with the baby after things have settled down a little.

If you continue to have difficulty bonding with your baby, consider going to therapy to resolve some of the issues from your past and to learn how healthy families meet their children's emotional needs.

Don't underestimate the power of kindness. All parents will make mistakes. It's inevitable. If you love your children and treat them with kindness, they are likely to do just fine in life. Children are resilient and forgiving. They will be unharmed by minor parenting mistakes but will struggle in life if they don't feel that you love them.

How do you know if you love them enough? Pay attention to your feelings when your children are misbehaving. Do you feel angry and frustrated but still love them? Do you think about how they feel and are careful not to say mean things to them or hurt them even though you're so angry you feel like you could explode? If you answered "yes" to those questions, then you probably love them enough.

Never be unkind to your children. We've all had times when we've wanted to do or say something that wasn't very nice or even could be considered mean. No doubt there have been times when you've felt angry and even fantasized about acting out your aggression. You may have wanted to slap the person who just cut in front of you in line at the grocery store or given your boss a piece of your mind for assigning you too much work or passing you up for a promotion. But, chances are good you didn't act on those aggressive thoughts.

Why don't we act out our aggressive thoughts? First of all, we know there are consequences for our behavior (we might get fired or arrested). And we have been socialized to behave appropriately. Most of us would feel embarrassed and ashamed if we behaved aggressively in public. We all have certain lines we do not cross. For example, no matter how angry we feel, we refrain from striking someone or saying something nasty to a person who is in a position of authority.

The legal system sets many of the parameters for our behavior. For example, we know it's a crime to strike an adult and that child abuse and neglect are illegal, but the issue is far more complicated than that.

What behavior is and isn't acceptable varies in different families. Some parents never shout, no matter what. Others feel it is okay to yell occasionally but never acceptable to say demeaning things to their children. Many parents feel it's okay to spank their children, while others, including myself, feel that parents should never hit their children even as a form of discipline.

So where do you draw the line? I think you start by looking at how you interact with adults. Would you say demeaning things to your best friend? Of course, you would not. If you wouldn't treat your friend that way, is it okay to say mean things to your child? I don't think so. That's a line you just don't cross. Your children deserve to be treated with compassion and respect just like you and every other person does.

Ask yourself, "Am I comfortable with my child crossing that same line?" If your answer is "no," you draw the line there. If you behave in a certain way, your children will imitate that behavior. If you hit your child, chances are good he'll strike out at his friends, siblings, and probably even you occasionally. If you swear, your child probably will swear on occasion as well. Decide where you want to set the boundaries and then insist that your child, like you and the other members of your family, never cross those lines. Remember, though, you can't expect your child to control her behavior if you can't control your own.

Model kindness. Children learn to be kind and compassionate by experiencing it first hand. Give your children hugs and kisses, say kind things to them, share with them, give them your undivided attention, tell them what you love most about them, compliment them, and spend time having fun with them.

Unfortunately, many parents weren't treated kindly as children. How do you know how to be a loving parent if your parents were neglectful or abusive? You can read parenting books or magazines, go to family resource centers, take a parenting class, or go to individual or group therapy. Watch how those of your friends who you consider to be good parents deal with their children. Listen to how they talk to and how they show affection towards their children.

Encourage your child to practice kindness through play. Commercials tell us to buy electronic toys for our kids. I'm not opposed to them, but make sure your children also have access to toys like baby dolls and stuffed animals. Kids have wonderful imaginations. Their teddy bear doesn't need to play taped responses to them or dance when your child presses a button. Buy your child a basic teddy bear or other stuffed animal. Encourage him to tuck his bear into bed at night and give him hugs when he feels that his bear is sad or lonely. Praise him when he's being kind. You could say, "You take such good care of your bear. I bet he loves those giant hugs you give him."

Consider getting a family pet. Kids learn a great deal from their pets. Pets teach them to be responsible and give them opportunities to form attachments and to practice being affectionate. Pets can teach children to be gentle, kind, and loving. For example, if your child pulls the cat's tail, the cat will run away or snarl at her. But if she pets her nicely, the cat is likely to sit with your child for hours. Pets are forgiving and have endless amounts of unconditional love to give to children.

If you do decide to get a pet, make sure your child is old enough to treat it kindly. Spend the time to teach him how to hold his hamster gently or play with the dog without hurting it. Be prepared to provide most of the care for the pet until your child is mature enough to take care of him.

When I was growing up, I had horses. I spent hours brushing them, talking to them, cleaning their stalls, and feeding them. They weren't just animals to me. I formed attachments with each of them, and they became important members of my family and significant relationships in my childhood.

Make sure your children are treated with kindness. It's hard to teach your children to be kind to others if you allow people to mistreat them. Tell your child that everyone deserves to be treated kindly. If your son comes home and tells you he's being bullied in school, ask him for details. Then contact his teachers or guidance counselor and insist they take action to put a stop to the bullying immediately. If necessary, contact the bullies' parents and, if the bullying continues, contact the school principal or superintendent or possibly the police.

Tell your child she doesn't have to be kind to everyone. Kindness is a two-way street. Most of us were raised believing we should always be nice no matter what. That resulted in problems for some kids and is probably not the message you want to give to your children. Let them know they don't have to be nice to someone who's trying to pull them into a car, molest them, or steal their lunch money. Give them permission to kick, punch, and bite anyone who tries to abduct them. Let them know they can stand up to the bullies at school and tell them what they really think of them.

Teach your children to see people as people, not objects. Too often, we refer to people as objects. We use labels to identify them and forget they are people with dreams, needs, and feelings like us. How often have you heard people use the term hobo? Kids see hoboes as funny characters and may want to dress up like them for Halloween. I was mortified when I went on a fifth grade class trip with my daughter, Megan. The bus stopped at a light and one of the boys in her class yelled, "Look it's a hobo." Kids quickly gathered at the windows to see a "hobo." They didn't realize he might have been a homeless veteran who returned from the war to no job and no place to live or perhaps he was a person struggling with mental illness. They definitely saw him as someone very different from themselves and didn't consider how difficult his life must be.

Give your children opportunities to meet people who struggle. Take them to volunteer at a soup kitchen or introduce them to one of your co-workers who has a disability.

When I was a kid, children with handicaps were bused to other schools, but today children with disabilities are integrated into regular education classrooms. My daughter, Megan, and all her classmates were taught sign language so they could communicate with a classmate who had a hearing impairment. They took turns helping another classmate who had severe physical and cognitive disabilities. She couldn't speak, but Megan and her classmates learned to communicate with her and enjoyed making her laugh.

Encourage your children to walk in other people's shoes. We all try to avoid thinking about things that make us feel bad, and children are no exception. It's easier for them to make fun of the child with a handicapping condition than to empathize with her. If your child is laughing at the homeless man living on the streets, talk with her about how sad it is that he doesn't have a bed to sleep in or a home in which to live. If she is laughing about a youngster who looks different from his peers, ask your child how she would feel if kids were laughing at her.

Give the message that they should be kind because it makes people feel good, not because they might get into trouble if they're mean. Years ago, children where told that bad things would happen to them if they were unkind. The message was that good people go to heaven when they die and bad people go to hell. Comments like, "You'd better not pick on your brother or you're going to be in big trouble" were common. Adults meant well but could have used better strategies to mold children into caring and compassionate adults.

The problem with threats of punishment is that they don't work when the child knows that no one is watching and the chances of getting caught are slim. A better strategy to use is to praise children for acts of kindness. Comments like, "I'm so proud of you. You were kind to Tim even though your friends were telling you to be mean to him" or "Did you see the smile on her face when you helped her? You're such a great kid" go so much further in creating kind children than threats of punishment ever will.

Seek help for your child if he's cruel to animals. When children are small, they sometimes inadvertently hurt animals. That's nothing to be alarmed about, but you should be concerned if your older child deliberately harms animals, especially if she seems to get pleasure from doing so. Take your child to a therapist if she kills the family cat or sets the dog's hair on fire. That kind of behavior usually indicates the child has a more serious problem that needs to be addressed as soon as possible. Don't ignore the problem. Without treatment, it won't go away.

Teach your children how to be nice. It's true that children are naturally kind. Babies and toddlers have smiles, hugs, and kisses that melt your heart, and children jump at the opportunity to help others. Talk to your children about the many ways they can be nice. Explain that little things like holding the door open for others, sharing lunch with a child who forgot her lunch money, smiling at someone who seems a little sad, and inviting a child to sit with them at lunch can change someone's day from terrible to wonderful. When your child performs some act of kindness, even if it's just a little thing, comment on it. Let him know you admire his ability to be kind to others.

Help your child understand that actions such as being on time, writing thank you notes, sharing, talking positively about friends even behind their backs, and following through on promises are all ways we treat others with kindness.

Teach your child to say kind things to others. Expressing kindness to others doesn't come easily for everyone, especially for children who have attachment issues and may be afraid to get close to others. This is a common problem for children who were adopted as they mature. Explain to your child it's okay to tell someone you love him and that people like to hear comments such as: "I missed you when you went away." "You're my best friend." "You did a great job." Make sure you say kind things to your children. Tell them you love them, you think they're special, and that you are so glad they were born (or that you adopted them).

Encourage your child to be kind even when others aren't. Kids can be cruel. Children worry about being teased and sometimes in order to protect themselves will join their peers in ridiculing another child. By the time your child reaches middle school, you should have conversations with her about bullying. Make it clear you won't tolerate bullying and that you expect her to stand up for people who are being mistreated.

Set very clear limits when it comes to being cruel to others. Take the cell phone away if he's sending mean texts and cut off Internet access if he's writing derogatory comments about peers on social networking web sites. If he does something unkind to a peer, let him know you're extremely disappointed with him and ask him why he would do something to a friend or classmate that could be hurtful. Tell him you expect him to apologize and be kinder in the future.

Make sure you protect your child from mistreatment by others. If another child is being cruel to your child, discuss ways he can cope with the situation. Role-play ways to respond in an assertive manner. Tell him to look the person in the eye and say in a clear, loud tone of voice to stop saying hurtful things to him. Pretend to be the abuser and have your child practice standing up for himself. Encourage your child to try to resolve the situation on his own, but if that doesn't work, intervene on your child's behalf.

Provide opportunities for your child to be kind to others. Children love to care for others even if they won't admit it. As a member of the cheerleading team, my youngest daughter had to volunteer to serve dessert to elderly people at a church dinner. She complained about having to go but came home talking about how much the people appreciated her help. It boosted her self-esteem and made her feel more comfortable interacting with elderly people.

Most teachers are great about providing opportunities for students to help others. Our school has fifth graders serve as reading buddies for kindergarten students. Each fifth grader is asked to take a turn carrying lunch for children in wheelchairs, and one child per week per class is assigned to be the teacher's helper. All of those activities help kids see themselves as kind people and learn they can have a positive impact on others.

Never tell your children they're bad. Kids don't need to hear comments like "you're a bad boy." If you dislike their behavior, tell them that. Say, "I don't like it when you hit" and then explain how you expect him to behave. You might add, "If you're angry, tell Johnny you're angry but don't hit him." Let your child know the behavior may be bad, but that doesn't make him a bad person. This may seem trivial, but it's not. Children who repeatedly hear they are bad people begin to believe it. Explain to your children that everyone has the potential to do both good and bad things. You could say, "You are a very nice person, but I don't like the way you talk about your friends behind their backs. That's not very nice, and I doubt you would want your friends to talk about you behind your back."

Help your children incorporate positive things about themselves into their self-image. Sometimes kids don't realize their worth. They may see themselves as good athletes or great students but fail to recognize that they're kind to others, willing to share, or a wonderful friend. Point out how nice you think they are. Kids love to hear things like, "You're my buddy. I love to go fishing with you" or "You're such a sweetheart."

Help your children understand we all have good and bad qualities. Healthy adults have well-integrated personalities. They accept that their personality consists of good and bad qualities. Help your child understand that her behavior may be mean spirited at a given time, but she's still a good person. To reinforce this you might say, "I think your comment was mean when you told Sarah she's ugly. You're a nice person, but that behavior is not nice at all, and I don't like it."

Questions to Ponder

Take a few minutes and think about yourself.

- Do you see yourself as kind to others or is that something you should work on improving about yourself?
- How about your parents? Were they kind and nurturing to you? If not, was there someone else in your life who was nurturing such as a teacher, neighbor, relative, or coach?
- What acts of kindness did they demonstrate?

Now think about how you treat your children.
- Are there lines you don't cross?
- Do you nurture your children even when you are tired and would rather focus on your own needs?
- Do you wish you could be more supportive of your children or feel that you may not have bonded with them as well as you should have?
- Do you feel you need help to become a better parent to your children or have issues from your own childhood you still need to work through? If so, have you contacted a therapist and made an appointment or signed up for a parenting class?

— NOTES —

CHAPTER 7

BEHAVIOR

I don't think people can talk about children for long without somehow discussing behavior. We often hear or say things like: "She's a great kid. She's so well behaved." "He used to fool around a lot in class, but he's much better this year." Or "I don't like her behavior when she's around those older kids."

We all had our opinions about parenting and children's behavior before we had children of our own. I don't think there are many, if any, of us who didn't watch a child throw a tantrum in the grocery store or hear a teen talk back to her parents and think *my kids aren't going to act like that.* Then we had our own children and discovered that being a parent isn't quite as easy as it looks.

Teaching our children how to behave appropriately is much more challenging than it appears. Behavior is complex. It serves many functions and is triggered by a range of internal and external factors. Behaviors that are desirable in one situation may be considered horribly inappropriate in another. For instance, joking with teammates is fine at the pizza party after a ball game but not okay in the middle of math class. Cultures and families also have their own definitions of acceptable behavior. For example, a girl in one family may be able to hang out with the boys in the neighborhood, while one from another family may not be permitted to talk to a boy on the phone without a parent listening in on the call.

Age also defines what behaviors will be tolerated. It's acceptable for a toddler to suck his thumb but definitely not a teen. We cringe at the sight of a five-year-old performing seductive moves in a dance recital but may be more tolerant when those same dance steps are performed by an older teen.

To complicate matters, children look to adults to learn how to behave. Unfortunately, our culture is full of adult role models who behave badly. We can't turn on the news without learning about a white-collar criminal stealing his investors' money or hearing about a person who committed a robbery or murder. Television is full of reality shows glamorizing drug use, promiscuity, and outrageous behavior. It's nearly impossible to go to a public place these days without seeing some type of inappropriate behavior.

Many kids are living in homes where adults don't behave appropriately. My oldest daughter was upset in elementary school when her classmates began talking about their lives at home. She heard stories of parents being drunk or using drugs, becoming violent, and spending time in jail.

To complicate things even further, behaviors can trigger intense emotions in parents. For example, if your older brother used to beat you up as a kid, chances are good that you're going to become angry if you see your oldest child hitting his younger sibling. No matter how hard you try to remain neutral, the truth is there will be times when your children's behavior really pushes your buttons. You may be mortified to learn that your daughter just sent a nasty e-mail to a classmate or that your son got into a fight at school. You may struggle to control your own anger when your child deliberately defies you or says something mean to you during an argument.

So how do you handle behavior problems when they occur and raise your children to behave appropriately?

Facts about Behavior

Children will misbehave. It's a fact of life. All children test our limits, become grouchy when they're tired or sick, struggle to express their emotions appropriately, and make mistakes. Don't be too hard on them or yourself. Try to view behavior problems as opportunities for learning and discussion. When your child has a tantrum in the grocery store because she missed her nap, take a deep breath, relax, and remind yourself that every parent watching has been in your shoes at one time or another. When your teen does something you don't approve of, use it as an opportunity for learning and try to remember that you probably made a mistake or two when you were his age.

Model appropriate behavior. We all know this, but it can't be said enough. Your children aren't going to do what you say. They're going to do what you do. If you go out drinking every Friday night, your teen probably is going to spend his weekend nights partying, too. If you text while driving, don't be surprised if your teen does the same when she starts driving.

Small children are notorious for imitating their parents' behavior. It's inevitable your children will dress up like you and imitate your every word and gesture. When your child mimics you, sit back, watch him, and think about the behaviors he's displaying. Then ask yourself if those are the behaviors you want him to learn.

Children often use behavior to communicate. Learning to behave appropriately is incredibly challenging but nowhere as difficult as learning to communicate effectively with words. Think about anger. When a child is angry with a friend, she needs to recognize that she's angry, find the words to express her feelings, and then be able to look her friend in the eye and tell him how she feels. This is difficult and most youngsters find it easier to hit or push their peers.

Misbehavior can reflect an infinite number of feelings that kids have difficulty expressing with words such as sadness, illness, pain, exhaustion, frustration, anger, love, and fear.

Behavior can serve many functions. Your child might act out to attract attention, pretend to be sick in order to stay home from school (especially if she can't do the work or is being bullied), suck her thumb in an effort to soothe herself, take risks to fit in with peers, or use drugs to distract herself from intense, emotional pain. Often children aren't even aware of the function of the behavior. For example, your child might be unaware she misbehaves in order to get your attention or acts out in class so her teacher won't ask her to read aloud.

Pay attention to sudden or severe changes in behavior. No one knows your child better than you do. Trust your intuition and take major changes in behavior seriously as they usually indicate something is wrong. Your fussy infant may have a fever or be in pain. Your older child may refuse to go to school because her peers are bullying her. And the fact that your teen has started lying and being secretive may indicate he's using alcohol or drugs.

Be particularly attentive if you notice a change in behavior when your child is around a particular individual. For example, has she been crying at day care ever since a new aide began working in her classroom or having tantrums when you try to leave her with a new sitter? We'd all like to believe that adults will always treat our children kindly, but unfortunately that's not always the case.

Behavior problems may indicate that your child is stressed. Childhood is not the carefree time it seemed to be years ago. Many kids have far too many demands on them and struggle to cope with daily stressors. To avoid feeling guilty, parents sometimes avoid noticing the effects of stress on our children. For instance, you may try to convince yourself that occurrences like divorcing your spouse, working extra hours, or struggling financially are not having a negative impact on your children when, in fact, they are.

How do you know your children's lives are becoming too stressful? They may become irritable, get angry easily, seem anxious or nervous, withdraw from activities or spend less time playing with friends, have difficulty sleeping or concentrating, or cry frequently. One child in your family may respond to stress one way, while her sibling may respond to it very differently.

Talk to your children about their behavior. It can be difficult for children to identify their emotions, understand what's bothering them, and express their concerns in words. If they're having behavior problems, sit down together and ask them if something is wrong. Sit quietly, listen, give them a chance to express their emotions, and don't try to "make everything better." Let them know it's okay to cry, get angry, and talk about sad, frightening, or embarrassing topics. Try to be patient and pay close attention to what they're saying and how they're feeling. Validate their feelings. For example, you could say, "You sound really mad. I think I'd be mad, too, if my friend did that to me."

Keep in mind that if your children don't have a way to talk about and cope with their feelings, they are likely to express them through negative behavior. For example, if you discourage your son from crying and expressing sadness, he may become depressed and withdrawn. If you prevent your daughter from yelling and expressing her anger, she may turn her anger inward and engage in self-injurious behavior such as cutting.

Don't underestimate the role of not enough sleep in behavior problems. Everyone gets grumpy and irritable when they're tired. Parents do and so do kids. Unfortunately, too many kids don't get enough sleep. We let them stay up too late to watch a favorite TV show or don't realize their bedtime is too late, and they're just not sleeping enough each night. When kids are tired, they're likely to become irritable, angry, and easily frustrated. They'll have trouble concentrating in school and may cry, whine, or act out aggressively.

Ask your pediatrician how many hours of sleep your child should get each night but remember every child is different. My youngest daughter can get by on seven or eight hours of sleep a night, but her older sister becomes irritable if she has less than eight or nine hours of sleep a night. As parents, we know our infants and toddlers need to sleep a lot, but sometimes we don't realize how important sleep is for our adolescents. Their brains are growing and teens require a lot of sleep, often more than they needed when they were a little younger. Parents may think their teens are being lazy when they sleep late on the weekend, but that's usually not the case. Most adolescents need to use the weekends to catch up on their sleep.

Set clear expectations for your kids. One of the biggest mistakes parents make is to not give clear direction to their children. For example, it isn't helpful to tell them you want them to behave on the field trip to the museum. Instead, explain to them what behavior is and is not appropriate in that type of setting. Encourage them to ask questions, but let them know it's not okay to goof around, run, yell, or touch things that are in roped-off sections or have "Do not touch" signs in front of them.

Also, remember that kids don't have the best memories in the world. It is helpful to make a list of the chores you want them to complete before they go to the movies with friends. You might remind them to fill up the gas tank on their way home every time they take the car rather than to assume they'll remember something you told them a week ago. Often we assume that kids deliberately chose not to do something, when the truth may be they just forgot.

Encourage your children to tell the truth. All children will misbehave, but not all of them will admit to their mistakes and take responsibility for their actions. Some children begin lying at an early age and continue throughout their lives.

How you respond when your child misbehaves significantly influences the likelihood she will tell the truth. The fact is a child is not going to admit to doing something wrong if doing so results in severe punishment. You need to make it worth her while to tell the truth. For example, you can say, "I'm mad that you didn't listen to me and spilled the red juice on the living room carpet, but because you told the truth and admitted you were the one who spilled it, I'm going to let it go this time."

Reward positive behaviors. Punishment is not what molds a child into a respectable adult. What really makes a difference is reinforcing desired behaviors. Reinforcers are tangible goods, responses, or events that when received following a behavior increases the likelihood that the child will exhibit that behavior again. If saying "Great job" after your child cleans her room encourages her to clean it again, then your praise is a reinforcer. The same is true for all sorts of things such as money, attention, gifts, opportunities to participate in an enjoyable activity, food, etc. Something that is reinforcing for one person, though, may not reinforce another person's behavior. One child may study hard to earn his parent's praise, while their approval may have little or no impact on whether or not his sister studies.

Tangible reinforcers should be used sparingly and always in conjunction with a social reinforcer such as a smile, praise, or a hug. For instance, ideally your children should do their homework because they like to learn and take pride in their academic achievement, not because you'll pay them five dollars to do it. Strange as it may seem, sometimes too many tangible reinforcers, like money, can actually decrease some children's motivation to get good grades.

Make sure you reward good behavior far more often than you punish bad behavior. If you take your child's phone away for talking back to you, make sure you praise him when he's behaving more appropriately. Praise your children when they do good things. Avoid just saying, "Good job," but specify what behavior you're reinforcing. "You did a great job. You studied hard this quarter and really pulled up your math grade."

Teach alternative responses to negative behaviors. Sometimes kids display negative behaviors because they don't know of more appropriate ways to behave. Your toddler may yank toys out of her peers' hands because she hasn't learned how to use words to ask for them. Your middle school son may smoke with the other boys in the neighborhood because either he doesn't know how to say "no" to his peers or lacks the self-confidence to stand up to peer pressure.

Talk to your children about ways to obtain attention without acting out. Encourage them to ask for help in school instead of avoiding homework they find too difficult. Make sure you pay attention to them when they ask appropriately for assistance. Help them learn how to ride a bike, play a sport, or make a craft so they don't spend their free time fighting with their sister or jumping on the furniture.

Behavior shouldn't be the focus of your relationship with your child. Think how incredibly fortunate we are to be able to raise children. They enrich our lives in ways most of us never imagined, but, unfortunately, our children grow up way too fast. Don't waste these precious years focusing on the negative. Attend your children's activities and have a blast watching them grow into interesting people. Enjoy playing and laughing with them and set aside time to do those little things that can mean a lot to both of you such as walking on the beach, reading stories, or talking together.

Listen to the way you describe your child to others. When you describe your son to a co-worker, do you focus on negative behaviors or talk about him in positive terms? Do you say, "He's always getting into things, never seems to finish anything he starts, and now is flunking math" or "He's a great artist and has such a great sense of humor."

Keep your expectations realistic. Sometimes parents set expectations that are too high for their children or fail to match them to their child's developmental age or temperament. A toddler is not going to sit quietly while her parents talk with friends for several hours, a hyperactive child is not going to sit in a class taught by a boring teacher without getting fidgety, and most three-year-olds can't watch their siblings open birthday presents without feeling jealous.

So what do you do? One thing you can do is to make situations more tolerable for your child. Explain to your three-year-old that he'll have another birthday in a few months, but then get him a small gift, too. Ask your child's current teacher which teacher he should have the following year and then request that person. Most teachers will say something like, "Jason learns better when he's active. I think Mr. Jones is the best match for him because he uses hands-on activities to teach skills." If you are going to dinner at a friend's house, bring activities for your child to work on and take breaks to read him a short book or take him for a walk around the block.

Provide consequences for problematic behaviors. As parents it's our job to teach our children to behave appropriately to help them fit comfortably into society. Everyone, including us, has consequences for his or her bad behavior. If you speed down the road, you're going to be stopped and forced to pay a fine. If you show up late to work, refuse to do your work, or shout at your boss, you may end up getting fired. If you fail to pay your mortgage, you'll lose your house. You get the point.

Children need to have consequences for their bad behavior, too. If they don't, they're going to struggle to fit into society as adults. They may have difficulty holding a job, maintaining relationships, supporting themselves and their families, and possibly even staying out of jail.

But what kind of consequences should they have for bad behavior? The best answer is that the consequence should be appropriate for the transgression and the one most likely to lead to an improvement in behavior. Try to match the consequence with the function of the behavior. If your child breaks his cell phone deliberately, insist he pay for the replacement himself. If she yells at you when she wants your attention, say, "I'm not going to talk to you when you're yelling at me like that. You need to talk to me nicely." Make sure you stop and pay attention to her when she asks in an appropriate way.

If your son continues to run around the pool even though you've told him several times that running is dangerous and he has to walk, tell him swim time is over. You don't need to be harsh. The spare the rod and spoil the child mentality is a thing of the past. You don't need to hit, scream at, or belittle your children, nor should you. Just be consistent. Provide consequences for problematic behaviors and opportunities for your children to learn appropriate ways to have their needs met.

Be forgiving. Children do need to have consequences for bad behavior, but they also need to have kind, compassionate parents. If your child misbehaves, be willing to forgive and forget. For example, if your child opens your jewelry box and accidentally breaks a watch, let her know you're angry she disobeyed you because your jewelry box is off limits, but don't hold it over her head. Assume that after you've dealt with the issue, she'll behave differently in the future. Avoid starting off the next day with something like, "I hope you don't plan to get into my jewelry again today." Instead, start the day with a smile and some friendly words like, "You look nice today, Honey."

Set limits. Children need limits. Limits provide kids

with a sense of safety and security and let them know they can count on their parents to make sure they're okay. Deciding what limits to set is one of the most difficult tasks parents face. There are no easy answers for this because there is so much variably between children. One child may need to have close supervision in order to behave appropriately, while another can be given more independence. If you have more than one child, don't be surprised if each of them needs different limits and different amounts of structure and supervision.

Pick your battles. One thing all parents learn quickly is the need for flexibility. If you're tired, your child's tired, and you've both had a busy day, you may choose not to insist that your son empty the dishwasher before he goes to bed. Consistent but flexible is a healthy mix.

If your toddler is having a bad morning, pick your battles. Yes, you're going to insist she sit in her car seat as you drive her to day care, but you may choose not to fight with her about wearing clothes that match. Just explain to her day care provider she's having a rough morning and the strange color combination was her choice, not yours. Anyone who is a parent will understand.

Your child needs you to be a parent, not a friend. Your children may tell you they want you to be their friend, but in the long run they'll love you more if you behave like a parent rather than a peer. Recently, I heard of some parents getting drunk with their middle school-aged kids. At the time, perhaps they were popular with their children, but I wonder how the children will feel about their parents years from now if they're arrested for drunk driving or end up struggling with an addiction. My guess is they'll be angry and wish their parents had been more responsible.

Work with your child's teacher. Your child's teacher is going to have a significant impact on your child's life. Think about it. Mondays through Fridays during the school year, your child will spend as much, if not more, of his waking hours with his teacher as he spends with you. His teacher will inevitably share her views of life with him, respond positively or negatively to his behavior, and significantly impact how he views himself. She can make him feel like a brilliant student or wonderful friend or leave him wondering if he has what it takes to go to college or if he is less important than his peers.

Try to keep your child's teacher informed. Share information about important events happening at home that may impact his behavior and the comments he makes about school. Let her know he's frustrated with reading or feels the other kids don't like him. Ask her how the two of you can work together to help him gain confidence and self-esteem, as well as learn social and academic skills.

Ask the teacher for her input and be willing to take her concerns seriously. It's possible your daughter may be very well behaved at home but disrespectful in school when she has the attention of her peers and is out from under your watchful eye. Don't immediately discount her teacher's concerns. Yes, there's a possibility the teacher may have a negative opinion of your child that isn't accurate, but it's also possible she has information about your child and her behavior you need to hear.

Engage in ongoing discussions about behavior as your children grow up. Behavior is very complex. Most adults have times when they don't behave appropriately or wonder what behavior is expected in various situations. Maintain an open discussion with your children about behavior. Talk to them about things like peer pressure, what behavior is expected in various situations, and the consequences of displaying various behaviors or violating social norms or laws. Riding in a car is a great time to talk about these sorts of things, especially with teens.

Provide opportunities for your children to learn and practice positive behaviors. Occasionally children are deliberately defiant or oppositional, but usually their behavior is designed to meet their needs. For instance, a toddler who colors on the wall is not trying to make his parent angry. He's just having fun exploring his world and being creative. This problem can be solved simply, not by hitting the child, but by giving him appropriate places to draw. Hang a chalkboard on the wall or cover a table with paper and give him some crayons to use. Then make sure you're with him when he has access to the crayons so you can teach him to use them appropriately. Recognize his needs and channel his behavior in appropriate directions.

If your child is jumping on the furniture, consider buying a trampoline with a net around it and allow her to jump to her heart's content. If she tugs at your shirt and demands your attention when you arrive home from work, try waiting a half hour before starting dinner and spend that time talking with her.

Take responsibility for your role in a problem. Sometimes we are quick to blame our children for their behavior problems but forget to take a look at our own behavior. For instance, if your child colors on the wall, ask yourself if maybe you should have been watching her more closely. If he is demanding when you come home from work, take a close look at yourself and see if possibly you need to be more attentive with your children. Sometimes parents wonder why they should change their own behavior when it is their child who is acting out. There are several answers to that question.

First of all, it's the right thing to do. If we want our children to take responsibility for their behavior, we need to be willing to do the same. It also can make life easier for both you and your child. You might be surprised to find that a minor change, like giving your child extra attention when you arrive home from work, can prevent tantrums and reduce both your child's stress and your own.

Teach your children they aren't the only people in the world. Many behavior problems are the result of children feeling they aren't getting their needs met. The reality is there are many people in the world, and our needs can't always come first.

Babies' needs have to be met. You can't leave your infant crying in the crib because you want to stay in bed or haven't finished eating your dinner. But as children grow up, you do need to slowly teach them that their needs must be weighed against the needs of others. Sometimes you'll be on the phone and your child will have to wait for you to give him the attention he wants. Other times you won't be able to meet his need at all. For instance, he may need to understand that, although he would love to have a new video game, you just can't afford to buy it for him.

Don't give your children everything they want the minute they want it. We already have enough narcissists in the world.

Sometimes it can be hard to say no to our kids, especially if as children we didn't have our own needs met or if we grew up in poverty. If that's true for you, it may be a real challenge for you to refrain from over-indulging your children. Guilt can drive parents to spend too much money on their children. For instance, parents who feel guilty about divorcing a spouse may try to take their child's sadness away by buying him anything he wants. Unfortunately, money will never fill an emotional void or take away emotional pain. It just becomes a band-aid on top of an untreated wound.

Help your children learn to consider the needs of others by encouraging them to do volunteer work. As they get older, teach them the value of money and to take care of their belongings by insisting they get a job and start paying for some of their own things.

Some kids are just difficult to raise no matter how skilled their parents are at parenting. As parents, most of us can't help but compare our children to their peers. We see children sitting quietly in a restaurant and wish our children could be as well behaved. Or we watch a child acting out of control in a store and may look at the parents as the reason for the problem. Parenting does play a huge role in how our children behave, but it's not the whole picture. Some children are just much more difficult to parent than others. Some children tend to be quiet and enjoy sedentary activities while others have high energy levels and seem to always need to keep moving.

I remember watching an interview with Mary Lou Retton after she won her gold medal for gymnastics in the Olympics. She said that her mother signed her up for gymnastics because she wouldn't stop jumping on the furniture. If your child has a behavior you find particularly challenging, think about ways you might turn the problem into something more positive like Mary Lou's parents did.

Many children have neurological and temperamental factors that make it more difficult for them to acquire appropriate behaviors. For instance, parents of children with autism know that raising their children is more challenging than raising "typical" children. That's not to say they don't love their children and enjoy parenting them, but their jobs are especially demanding.

There are many factors that can make parenting more challenging. Some children have great difficulty controlling their impulses. Some get frustrated more easily than other children, act out their anger more aggressively, or have high levels of energy and seem to need to be moving all the time. Other kids are shy, tend to keep their feelings inside, frighten easily, are clingy, or demand a lot of attention. Try not to compare your child with other children or your parenting with other parents. Do the best you can given the circumstances, and don't be afraid to ask for help when you need it. Taking your child to a mental health provider or asking for help as a parent is nothing of which to be ashamed.

Watch for environmental factors that may be impacting your child's behavior. When our children misbehave, we tend to think the problem is either with the child or our parenting, but sometimes it's neither. Environmental factors such as food additives, noise, temperature, or even a dangerous neighborhood may play a role. For example, a child attending a school known for gang violence may become truant from school or pretend to be sick in order to stay home. My youngest daughter had times when she seemed to become very angry for no reason at all. Eventually we discovered she behaved that way whenever she ate foods with red dye in them such as the brightly colored strawberry milk she loved. We stopped giving her the milk and the angry outbursts disappeared.

Teach your children to control their own behavior. When your children are young, you have considerable control over their behavior. But as they grow older, they'll need to learn how to behave appropriately on their own. Young children may behave out of fear of being punished. But as they get older, they'll need to develop a conscience and behave, not because they might get caught, but because it's the right thing to do.

Encourage your children to take responsibility for their actions, praise them for taking initiative to complete a task without being asked or to do the right thing despite being pressured by peers to behave differently. Give them increasingly more independence and tell them you trust they'll make the right decisions. Talk to them about the importance of controlling their impulses and thinking before they act. Encourage them to express their feelings with words, not behaviors.

Questions to Ponder

Think about your childhood and how your parents taught you to behave appropriately.

- Do you think their strategies were effective or do you wish they had handled situations differently?
- Did they give you the skills you needed to succeed as an adult or did you find yourself struggling as a young adult?
- Was there an adult who had a significant impact on your life such as a teacher, coach, parent, or other relative? What did they teach you and how?

Now think about your children.

- What are some of the strengths and weaknesses each of them have?
- How do they respond in different situations and what skills have they acquired?
- What skills do they need to learn?
- Do they lie when they misbehave and, if so, what can you do to change their behavior?
- Are they becoming more independent and better

able to be trusted to behave responsibly even when you're not watching them?

- Are there factors that have a negative impact on their behavior?
- Do they tantrum when they're overly tired, act out in a particular class at school, or become more aggressive when playing with a certain child in the neighborhood?
- Have you talked to your children's teachers about their behavior? Do they have positive things to say about your children or concerns that may need to be addressed?
- Are you providing the parenting your children need to learn how to behave appropriately, even when it's easier to ignore problems when they occur?
- Are you enjoying being a parent or are your child's behavior problems making it difficult? Are you happy with the job you're doing as a parent?
- What could you do differently in order to become an even better parent than you currently are?

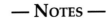

— NOTES —

CHAPTER 8

LEARNING

❧

Childhood is all about learning and growing. When they're young, children have to learn everything from how to hold their heads up without support and how to roll over in their cribs to how to ride their bikes, share their toys, and write their names. By the time they reach adulthood, they need to have acquired marketable skills, be able to maintain intimate relationships, manage their finances, clean their homes, and fill their free time with enjoyable leisure activities.

When we think about children and learning, we usually think about school and the academic skills our children need to learn, but that's only one small part of the learning taking place during childhood. As parents, we want to help our children develop their potentials to the fullest and find happiness and meaning in life. We want to help them identify their emotions, keep themselves healthy, communicate effectively, and develop a strong sense of self, to name just a few of the qualities they need to learn while they're growing up. We want them to develop a strong foundation for learning, one they can build on for the rest of their lives.

Nobody learns everything in life, not even close. But hopefully most of us master the skills that matter most to us and learn those things we need in order to live a meaningful and satisfying life. Like us, our children have numerous opportunities to learn. They can learn everything from self-destructive and harmful behaviors to skills that enable them to have a positive impact on the world around them. They can follow their dreams and learn how to climb a mountain, train a dog, paint a beautiful picture, play an instrument, become loving parents, perform surgery, or feed the poor. The options are endless.

Every child has different interests but also different abilities. Some kids seem to learn almost everything easily, while others struggle to grasp even basic concepts. But most children excel in some skills and find others difficult or even impossible to master.

We know that motivation plays a major role in learning. Children learn skills more easily when they are motivated to excel in those areas and are willing to practice regularly and continue to work at learning something even after they've failed. This is true for all children, even those who are particularly talented or gifted.

Fortunately, children have an innate love of learning, which makes our jobs as parents much easier. We don't need to be educators or know how to teach children all the things they need to learn. Primarily, we just need to protect their love of learning and provide them with opportunities to learn. If we provide them with support and make learning fun, children will do just fine in life.

Facts about Learning

Make sure your children have fun learning. Kids love to learn. Just listen to a preschooler for a few minutes, and you'll hear him asking endless questions as he tries to understand why things happen and how the world works. Take him to a children's museum, and he'll beg you to let him stay longer. If you stand near the nonfiction section in the library, you are sure to see kids eagerly searching for books on everything from how cars work to how to draw horses.

All children start out in this world loving to learn. Unfortunately, parents and teachers can destroy that desire. Your child's interest in learning will plummet if you ridicule her when she fails, force her to sit and study when she really needs some time to play, or pressure her to succeed so you can bask in her accomplishments as if they were your own. (Yes, no matter how hard you try to hide it, your child will know if you're trying to live your life vicariously through hers.)

Fortunately there are numerous ways you can ensure that your child retains his love of learning. You can teach him about measuring by baking a cake or building bookshelves together. You can improve his knowledge of science by finding a book about insects and then looking for them as you take a walk together in the woods or at your local park. If you own a dog, encourage your child to ask the veterinarian questions or to go on-line and learn about dog training or different breeds of dogs. You can send your kids to special camps, buy them books on their favorite topics, or provide opportunities for them to meet people who work in different fields.

Most importantly, though, you need to show a genuine interest in what your children are learning. Listen attentively as they tell you what they learned in school and tell them how proud you are of them. Comments like, "I'm amazed at how well you can speak French. I wish I could do that" or "You know so much about skateboarding. I'm glad you love it so much" can go a long way in helping your children retain their love of learning.

Never underestimate the power of modeling. Children are constantly learning from their parents and watch their every move. You might think your child is just tagging along while you run errands, but he is watching you closely and learning to behave just like you do. He might be learning how to handle conflict when someone cuts in line at the grocery store, the importance of saying "Thank you" to the cashier, or that it's okay to drive over the speed limit when you're late for a dental appointment. In similar situations, he's likely to use the same words he heard you say, imitate your body language and tone of voice, and even display the same emotions.

If you stayed calm when someone cut in front of you in line, he's likely to respond the same way in a similar situation. If you began to rant and rave, don't be surprised if you see him act the same way at some point in the future. If you walk out on your lover when you're angry, he may have difficulty remaining in a long-term relationship. If he sees you drunk frequently, he's likely to develop a drinking problem or grow up to be an alcoholic.

Encourage your child to discover her passion. We love to learn about things that interest us and the same is true for our children. You may be a chemist who has always loved science, but your daughter may love literature and dream of becoming a journalist or of writing novels. If that's the case, find opportunities for learning that would interest her, not you. Look on the Internet and find a camp for future journalists or a local writing or reading group for teens. Instead of a chemistry set for her birthday, consider giving her a gift card to a bookstore or buying her a laptop so she can start writing her first novel. Show her you're excited she is passionate about writing and encourage her to help you become a better writer or more knowledgeable about literature.

Ensure that your children have the support they need to succeed. We don't have fun learning when we're frustrated or continually failing. Your child isn't going to enjoy school if he can't see the board or hear what his teacher is saying. He'll hate to read if he doesn't receive help for his dyslexia and will dislike math if he has a teacher who can't teach math concepts well.

Children need many different types of support from parents in order to enjoy learning. They count on us to get them to bed on time so they aren't too tired to learn, to give them a good breakfast so they aren't hungry in English class, to get them extra help when they need it, and to intervene if they have a teacher who isn't kind to them or causes them to have an aversion to learning. Sometimes our kids will ask us to provide extra support, but not always.

Most younger children don't realize that staying up late will make it difficult for them to learn the next day. Many kids with learning disabilities aren't aware they have a disability or realize that's the reason they're earning poor grades. Instead, they may incorrectly believe they're stupid or don't work hard enough. As parents, it's our job to notice when our children need extra assistance and to do our best to get them the extra help they need.

Make sure your child's experience at school is positive. Meet with the teacher, guidance counselor, or school personnel if your child dislikes school, is saying he is repeatedly being teased or bullied, feels his teacher doesn't like him, or is saying things like, "My teacher thinks I'm stupid." Insist they take your concerns seriously and provide a positive, learning environment for your child.

Show your children you support them. Spend time helping them do their homework, make sure they have the supplies they need to complete class projects, and attend their school events. Talk to them about the struggles they'll face along the way and let them know it's okay to make mistakes. Explain to them that you want them to work hard and do their best, but you'll be there for them if they fail. Let them know you don't expect perfection and want them to feel comfortable talking to you about any concerns they have.

Advocate for your children. I always feel bad for children whose parents either don't or can't advocate for them. The truth is the world isn't always fair, and children whose parents advocate for them are more likely to benefit from opportunities in life than those whose parents aren't involved. Schools work within financial constraints and may not give your child the full range of extra services available to her unless you insist they do so. Guidance counselors are responsible for hundreds of students and may not think to inform your child she could attend college part time in her senior year, participate in a leadership program, or graduate a year early. Your child may not receive extra help with reading if you don't insist he be evaluated to see if he qualifies to receive help from a reading specialist.

I can't stress enough how important it is to form relationships with your children's teachers and to let them know you want to work with them to ensure that your children obtain a good education.

Give your child access to resources available today. Those of us who grew up before kids had cell phones and computers sometimes are wary of modern technology. We worry about the dangers our kids might encounter using these items, and some of us restrict our children's access to them. Certainly it's important to keep our children safe, but we need to remember that the world has changed. Our children need to be able to do research on the Internet and network with friends through social networking sites if they're going to be competitive in tomorrow's job market.

If you're uncomfortable with these new means of communication, educate yourself and be vigilant about ways to keep your children safe, but don't totally restrict them from using these tools. If you can't afford to buy some of the things your child needs for school, don't get discouraged. Many schools have musical instruments to loan to children who can't afford to buy their own and money to cover the cost of field trips for underprivileged children. Most schools also allow kids to come in before and after school to use the computers if their parents can't afford to purchase one.

Help your children understand that educational opportunities enrich their lives. Show your children that learning isn't some chore you complete like doing the dishes. Too often kids focus on "getting done with school" or learning things in order to pass a test or complete a course. Help them understand that learning enables us to become who we are and enriches our lives in ways that may not be immediately apparent. Explain to your children we never know where life will take us or what knowledge and skills we'll need to succeed.

For instance, a teen who takes German only to fulfill a graduation requirement may join the military and find himself stationed on a German Air Force Base. Another kid who doesn't want to learn math may be surprised at how much math he needs to succeed in his construction job. Talk to your children about things you wished you had learned when you were younger and how some courses you skipped would have come in handy later in life.

Model lifelong learning. It's important to show your children that learning isn't just something you do in school or when you're a child, but something that gives us a lifetime of enjoyment. Show them how learning can enrich their lives by continuing your own education. Take a painting class, join a writing group, learn to speak a foreign language or how to play a musical instrument. Or go back to school for a masters degree. Talk to your kids about the things you're learning and share your excitement about mastering new skills or reaching new goals.

Learn together with your kids. A great way to bond with your child is to take a class or learn a new skill together. My daughter, Megan, and I began riding lessons together about a month ago and love it. We enjoy spending time with each other as we drive to and from the barn, and we are both becoming better riders.

Take advantage of opportunities to learn from your children. Sometimes parents feel it is important to always be seen as the expert in their children's eyes, but that's not the case. When we let our children teach us, we give them the message we believe they're intelligent and talented individuals and we value their opinions. This is important. It improves their self-confidence and self-esteem and is the start of a relationship between you and your children that's built on mutual respect and admiration.

You'll be surprised how quickly your children will begin teaching you things. As babies and toddlers, they encourage us to play and have fun, teach us to be flexible, and remind us it's not all about us. As they grow older, the list of things we can learn from them is endless. My oldest daughter was only seven or eight when she pointed out that Pluto isn't a planet. It's a moon. Now that she's in high school, she talks to me about everything from the significance of historical events to the ideological views of past presidents. (I think I probably should have paid more attention in social studies when I was in school.)

Don't underestimate the value of family discussions during dinner. Some families do a really great job of using dinner time as an opportunity to both educate their children and bring the family closer together. They spend dinner talking about current events, sharing what they learned during the day, connecting on an emotional level, and engaging in healthy arguments. Kids in families who do this not only learn important facts but also learn how to hold their own in an argument. They can appreciate that people can have different perspectives on the same topic and that their opinions are just as valuable as anyone else's opinions.

Make sure dinner conversations are fun. Dinner isn't a time to ask children to recite facts or lecture them about the need to study more. Children should look forward to having dinner together as a family and not be afraid to have to answer a question or share an opinion.

Don't put too much pressure on your children. Today, kids face far too much pressure to succeed. Teachers push their students to excel on standardized tests, and by middle school kids begin hearing about the competition they'll face for admission into the college of their choice. That's on top of the pressure they impose on themselves as they try to reach their goals and perform better than their peers. This can be very stressful for all kids, but even more stressful for those who fear failure, have learning disabilities, or tend to be anxious.

Many kids face additional pressures, especially if they're following in the footsteps of a high achieving sibling or highly successful parent. It can be difficult for these kids to grow up hearing things like, "Aren't you Tom's sister? Wasn't he class valedictorian?" or "You're Dr. Smith's daughter. Are you going to be a doctor like your dad?" Let your child know that everyone is different and she'll make her own mark on the world. Point out her strengths and tell her how proud you are of her and all she has accomplished. For example, brag about her volunteer work as much as you boast about the fact her brother became class valedictorian. Tell your son that, although he may not excel in math like you did, you envy his ability to play baseball so well.

Encourage your children to play. Play is invaluable as a learning tool and such an important part of childhood. Kids learn gross motor skills when they run with friends, ride their bikes, shoot basketballs, or learn to ski. They develop their fine motor abilities as they draw, write, and dress their dolls. They improve their hand-eye coordination when they play video games and hit baseballs.

Children learn so much more though. While playing, they develop social skills, use their imaginations, learn to resolve conflicts, cope with anger, develop relationships, overcome fears, and master skills. They role-play being a parent, doctor, or firefighter as they try to define themselves and wonder who they'll become as they grow up. They try to figure out if they like to build bridges or care for sick animals. They develop feelings of confidence as they pretend to be super heroes.

Children are great at finding ways to have fun, but there are things you can do to help them benefit the most out of play time. For one thing, you can encourage them to engage in different types of play. If your son loves to play video games, encourage him to go outside and play tag with kids in the neighborhood or shoot baskets with his siblings. Help him find activities that help to develop his creativity and use his imagination. Make sure all of his toys don't talk or involve use of the computer or television.

Little children are great at treating stuffed animals like people. They give them names, personalities, and the ability to speak. Older children like to engage in imaginative play with dolls and action figures or put on plays for their parents.

Provide materials that will motivate your child to play. Rotate toys so your children can see new toys periodically. If you notice your kids have stopped playing with a particular game, tuck it away and bring it out again in a few months. Keep toys around that encourage creativity such as art supplies, musical instruments, or building blocks. You don't need to spend a lot of money. Children are more than happy to make art projects out of paper towel tubes, build playhouses out of empty boxes, or make music with pots and pans. Don't forget that what feels like work to you may seem more like play to your children. Kids love to help their parents paint a room, bake cookies, or even vacuum, sweep, or weed the garden. These activities are not only fun but also provide great opportunities for learning.

Try to help your children learn how to play with others but also to amuse themselves when they're alone. Encourage them to find pleasure doing things like reading, taking a walk in the woods or a park, or playing with the cat. It's important for kids to learn they don't need to spend every waking minute sending texts to their friends or talking on their cell phones.

Make it a priority to play with your children every day. Go outside and push them on the swings, ride bikes with them around the neighborhood, or play a board game together. Spend time reading with them every night and encourage your child to tell you jokes or sing silly songs with you. Believe me, you won't regret it. Before you know it, your children will be grown and you'll miss those times when your children wanted to play with you.

Children learn some things quicker from peers than from adults. Parents can be great teachers, but sometimes kids learn more easily from their peers than they do from adults. Your child may be struggling in his swimming class, but then suddenly start swimming in the family pool after watching his best friend swim under water. My daughter, Megan, was very frustrated with algebra and couldn't master some concepts even with extra help from her teacher. Then her sister, Rachel, worked with her for an hour, and she quickly learned the material.

So why do kids learn things so easily from peers? Sometimes children pay more attention to their peers, making it easier for them to learn a complex task, and it's possible kids may be more aware of how to explain something in a way that makes sense to a child. Often kids are just more confident and willing to take risks in the presence of a peer. They may think to themselves, he's watching me. I don't want him to think I'm a baby or if he can do it, so can I.

Kids have different learning styles. Good teachers recognize there are many different ways children learn and try to use several modalities to teach a concept. They may write about a topic on the white board, give the kids handouts to refer to later, and have the children work on projects in small groups. Good teachers recognize that some kids can't sit in a seat and pay attention for an hour at a time and often will plan activities that allow kids to get up and move around the room. They understand that many kids cope with learning disabilities such as dyslexia, attention deficit disorder, hearing and vision impairments and try to make sure all of the children are able to learn.

Help your child understand how she learns best. Ask her teacher for input and share it with your child. For example, tell her that her social studies teacher has noticed she learns better when she reads things rather than when she hears them. Encourage her to share this information with her other teachers. If your child is struggling with a particular subject, don't assume she isn't studying hard enough. That may be the case, but it's also possible the teacher needs to find a different way to present the information to your child or that your child needs tutoring.

Kids learn at different rates. When we have our first child, most of us can't help but read about the appropriate age for children to reach each developmental milestone such as rolling over, walking, and talking. It is important to know if your child's development is delayed and to share that information with his pediatrician so he can receive early intervention services if he needs them. But it's also important to remember that kids do learn at different rates. If you notice a delay, stay calm and share the information with her pediatrician. He will most likely recommend your child be evaluated and then will help you to find her additional help if needed. Many children with delays are able to catch up with the help of a physical, occupational, or speech therapist.

Recognize each child's strengths and weaknesses. Try not to compare your child to his sibling. All kids are different and have their own strengths and weaknesses.

Children are often very different from their parents. You may excel in math, but your child may be stronger in English or more geared towards a trade school rather than college. That's okay. There are lots of highly, successful people who didn't go to college but who have talents in other areas. One of your children may have the interest and math ability to become an engineer, while her brother may grow up to be a successful playwright.

Be careful not to try to turn your children into miniature versions of yourself. Appreciate them for who they are and help them gain skills in areas that match their strengths and interests. Make sure to compliment your children and let them know you value their strengths, even if they're very different from your own.

Secure extra help if your children need it. Parents may notice their child is struggling to learn but are afraid to share this with their student's teacher or to get her evaluated. They may remember children with disabilities being teased when they were in school. They may want to protect their child from teasing, be in denial the child has a problem, or be unaware of the importance of early intervention.

The earlier children are assessed and can begin receiving extra help, the better their prognosis. Some parents don't realize their children can be evaluated even when they're just infants or that the evaluations are free. (The evaluations are paid by the Department of Health when kids are babies and then by the local school system usually around age three.) When cognitive, motor, or speech deficits are identified, children are able to receive services at no cost to their parents. Therapists will come into the home or provide services at a day care center until the child is no longer in need of the intervention.

If your child is struggling to learn, ask your health department or school system to evaluate him. You may need to get a recommendation from your pediatrician in order to ensure you aren't charged for the evaluation. There are many problems that can have a negative impact on a child's ability to learn that can't be identified without specialized testing. Testing can reveal that a child can't understand the information he's hearing, is unable to remember what he's learning, has an attention deficit disorder, can't see what the teacher is writing on the board, or suffers from a learning disability such as dyslexia, to name just a few of the many disabilities that can cause developmental delays.

Be supportive if your child has a disability. Let your child know it's okay to have a disability. We live in a society where people strive to be perfect or at least try to give the impression they are. The reality is, though, no one is perfect. Most people are far from perfect. If your child is diagnosed with a disability, reassure him you'll help him obtain the assistance he needs to reach his potential. Explain to him that many successful people have learning disabilities and talk with him about your weaknesses.

Ask your child to think about his classmates. How many of them also have learning disabilities? How many others struggle with challenges such as coping with a medical problem or physical disability or growing up in a family coping with poverty, substance abuse, or divorce? Ask if he knows any children who live in a home where English isn't the primary language and encourage him to think about the challenges they face in school.

Don't be afraid to share your educational struggles with your child. Tell her if you have a math disability, didn't graduate from high school, or can't read. Children are understanding, and a conversation with your child about your academic challenges is likely to improve your relationship with her. Plus, learning difficulties should not be kept secret as if they're something to be ashamed of. Encourage your child to ask for help if he's doesn't understand something and point out that if he's having problems learning a concept, other kids probably are, too.

Find great teachers for your kids. Your child's school will probably tell you that you can't request a particular teacher, but that's not always true. When my children were in elementary school, we had to complete a form each year identifying any special concerns to be considered when assigning them a teacher for the next school year. It said, very clearly, on the form that parents could not request teachers. However, after talking with several parents of older children, I learned many parents did make requests and their requests were usually granted.

Most teachers are excellent, but occasionally you'll cross paths with one who perhaps should have chosen another occupation or just isn't a good match for your child. A negative educational experience can cause a child to dislike school, and you certainly don't want that to happen to your child.

If that's the case, intervene and try to have your child assigned to a new teacher, which can be challenging but it can be done. My husband and I were successful in getting Megan a new kindergarten teacher, but it wasn't easy. We had to meet with the principal and then wait several months while he made surprise visits to the classroom, talked alone with Megan, and saw for himself that the teacher's negative interactions with her were ruining her self-esteem and causing her to hate school.

Although you can sometimes have your child placed in a different class if necessary, it's much easier to make sure your child has a good teacher right from the start. You can either talk to a parent of an older child or ask your child's current teacher to recommend a teacher for the following year. His teacher may say something like, "I don't think it matters. Jason will do fine with any of them" or he may suggest a specific teacher. Some kids do have specific needs. For example, children with attention deficit disorder often need a teacher who is good at providing structure, a shy child may do best with a teacher who's warm and fuzzy, and a creative child may thrive when assigned a teacher who gives her room to think outside of the box.

Help your children become well-rounded people. Today we hear so much about the competition our kids will face being accepted into top colleges, not to mention law, medical, or graduate schools. But be careful not to take all of that too seriously. Sure, you want to help your kids to reach their goals, but there's so much more to a person than his test scores, grades, college degree, or profession. Help your children become well-rounded people. Sometimes parents encourage their kids to focus on a limited subject area, which leaves them with deficits in other areas. A future engineer will be a more interesting person if she's also knowledgeable about the arts or social sciences. A teen who wants to become a doctor shouldn't spend every summer at a science camp but should consider going to a sports camp or a program that gives him opportunities to travel and learn about other cultures.

As I'm sure you know, different activities use different muscles and different parts of the brain. Encourage your children to become involved in gross motor activities such as swimming, bike riding, or dance and fine motor activities such as painting, drawing, or building models. Make sure they take a range of subjects that help them develop different cognitive abilities such as math, art, music, and foreign languages.

Help your children develop social skills. Try to find opportunities for them to interact with peers, develop leadership skills, and learn to work cooperatively with others. Ensure that they have unstructured time with friends and are able to develop close relationships with their peers.

Give your children as many opportunities for learning as possible. Even when your children are little, expose them to all kinds different things. Look for a good day care center with stimulating activities or, if you're a stay-at-home parent, consider joining a play group or sending your child to preschool. Take advantage of community activities for kids, take them to places where they'll see different things and meet other children. Provide them with an interesting and stimulating environment, but don't over schedule them. Kids need to have opportunities, but they also need time to relax and just have fun.

Educational television shows are great for teaching children basic academic and pre-academic skills, but don't use them as free baby-sitting. Interact with your children, make sure you look directly at them when you're talking. Get down on the floor with your preschooler and help her stack her blocks or put a puzzle together. Go outside and push her on the swing or take her to the library and attend story hour with her.

Don't worry if you don't have much money and can't afford to pay for expensive preschool programs or buy a lot of educational toys for your children. Headstart programs are a great way for low-income families to ensure their children receive access to a good preschool program. Most communities offer parenting centers where children have free access to educational toys while parents can obtain information about how best to help their children learn.

As your children grow older, continue to look for educational opportunities for them. Sometimes parents think school will provide their children with all of the education they need until they're grown up, but that's certainly not the case.

There are many opportunities available to children today, and parents need to put in time and effort to make sure their children are able to benefit from them. I've found one of the best ways to learn about educational opportunities is to network with other parents, especially ones who are teachers or have older children. Ask them questions about available programs and activities in which their kids have participated. Parents love to share ideas with each other, and you'll be surprised what you'll learn (and even the friends you'll make). You'll hear about everything from how to get your child in an advanced class at school to how to access government grants for your children to study a critical language in a foreign country.

You may also want to research educational opportunities on the Internet and to speak with your child's teachers and guidance counselor. School personnel are usually aware of a wide range of educational opportunities available at your child's school, in the community, and even throughout the country and the world. My oldest daughter recently become bored with high school and wished she could do something different in her senior year. I had heard of local students attending college during their senior year, called the university, and learned how my daughter could become involved. Then I shared that information with several co-workers with teens.

Sometimes educational opportunities are closer than you think. Next time you change the oil on the car or the air filter on the furnace, consider asking your child to help you. Show your child how to sew on a button, fix a leaky faucet, cook dinner, or paint a room. Talk with her about what you do at work and bring her to Take Your Son/Daughter to Work Day if your place of employment participates in such a program.

Children need to be taught how to learn. Sometimes children struggle in school or lose interest in learning because they lack the skills they need to learn. Your child is likely to fail a social studies test if she doesn't take good notes or become frustrated with math if she doesn't do her math homework. She may have difficulty breaking tasks down into smaller parts and may need you to help her do that.

Today schools teach students how to take notes and organize materials. They stress the importance of doing homework and provide extra help to students who need it. Sometimes, though, kids with learning difficulties, attention deficit disorder, or who are disorganized continue to struggle. If this is true for your child, meet with his teachers and ask how you can help. You may need to help him organize his papers, make sure he completed all of his homework assignments, or place his completed assignments back in his folders every night so he's prepared for school the next day.

Parents play a significant role in their child's education. Even if your child is very bright, helping him succeed in school will still be time consuming.

When your children are little, it's important for you to talk to them, give them a stimulating environment, and teach them everything from how to write their names to how to count and identify letters and colors. As they grow older, you'll play a significant role in teaching them how to read and do simple math. They'll learn these things in school, but they are likely to struggle if you don't spend time helping them with their homework and reading assignments each night. You'll need to ensure they're studying for tests, bringing materials to school, and doing their homework. Talk with them about any problems they're facing, including difficulties getting along with teachers and peers. Help them think about what classes they should take and what they would like to do when they grow up.

It's important to make sure your children enjoy learning. Avoid nagging them to do their homework or keeping track of every little thing they do. If your child is performing well in school, let her worry about studying for her tests and completing her homework. A big part of growing up is learning to be responsible. If your child is earning good grades, you are doing a good job and can back off and give her more independence. Unfortunately, some parents, particularly those who are living vicariously through their children or are afraid to let their children grow up, will become overly involved in their children's education. This can cause a child to lose his motivation to learn or to gain independence in the future.

Don't be surprised if you're unable to tutor your children with everything. You may not have taken a particular course when you were young or have forgotten what you learned years earlier. Sometimes we don't understand the new way the material is taught. If that's the case and your child is having difficulty, contact your child's teacher and ask him if he can spend some extra time after school helping your child. Many teachers are happy to do that.

Help your children learn how to enjoy life. We want to live our lives to the fullest and help our children do the same. Just as your children need to learn how to study, they also need to be able to relax and have fun. Try to be a good model by enjoying your own life. Provide your children with opportunities to develop leisure skills such as riding a bike, swimming, or playing a sport. Encourage them to develop hobbies and spend time with friends. Make sure they see you enjoying yourself. Invite friends over for dinner, go to the movies, ride your bike, take up a new hobby, go to the spa for a massage, or take a relaxing bubble bath. Work with your children to plan a family vacation and make sure to schedule activities everyone, including yourself, will enjoy.

Teach your children life skills. Children need to learn an infinite number of skills during their lifetimes in order to live happy and healthy lives. They need to learn how to eat healthy meals, manage their money, and find an apartment or purchase a house. They need to acquire the habit of exercising regularly and to seek regular medical care. Some of these things are learned in school, but you'll need to teach them the rest.

Advise your children how to find answers to their questions. Life is so complex and none of us have all of the skills we need. Even if we can teach our children many things, the reality is we can't teach them everything. Plus, we won't be around forever.

Teach your kids how to find answers if they don't have them. Talk to your teens about times when people hire experts such as lawyers, accountants, inspectors, contractors, or financial experts. When your son gets his driver's license, take him with you to talk with the insurance agent to add him to your policy. When he's preparing to go to college, talk with him about the cost and work with him to find scholarships. If he needs to take out loans, show him how much his monthly payment will be and how long he'll need to make the payments.

Knowledge is useful only if you know how to use it. If you've watched the news lately, you know that many companies receive a thousand or more applications for a job. Graduating with great grades just isn't enough to enable your kids to land that first job. Talk to your children about the importance of networking. When they're in college, encourage them to work as a research assistant, to do an internship, or to select a course with a hands-on component rather than one where they just memorize facts.

Social skills are just as important as academic skills. In order to be happy in life, people need to be able to form intimate relationships, maintain friendships, and establish good working relationships with bosses and co-workers.

One of the best ways to teach social skills is to take advantage of opportunities for learning when they occur. For example, if your child is being nasty to his cousins at a family picnic, take him aside and talk with him. Point out that he is most likely hurting their feelings and they probably won't want to spend time with him if he continues to be nasty. Suggest some better ways to behave so his interactions will be more positive.

Let your children decide for themselves what they want to be when they grow up. One of the biggest mistakes you can make is to try to live your life through your child. If you wish you were a doctor, either work hard and go to medical school or mourn the fact you will never become one, but don't push your child into medical school in order to meet your own needs. Our children are individuals. They may share some of our interests but rarely all of them. Encourage your children to figure out who they are and to follow their own dreams.

It's important to recognize that today many people change careers. Your child may go to college to become an artist, work in that field for several years, and then go back to school to become a lawyer, major in business, or develop a trade. Let your children know it's not the end of the world if they choose the wrong career. They can learn from their mistakes and go into a different line of work.

We know more education correlates with a higher income during a person's lifetime, but college might not be the best route for every child to take. Encourage your child to develop marketable skills in a field he enjoys and recognize that he may get those skills in college, at a trade school, or by doing an apprenticeship.

Questions to Ponder

Think about all the things you've learned in life and how you learned them.

- Were you fortunate enough to have supportive parents and good mentors?
- Were you given opportunities to learn by participating in camps, accelerated classes, or educational programs?
- Did you have access to educational resources such as a local library, a tutor when needed, and adequate school supplies?
- Did your parents attend parent-teacher conferences and Meet the Teacher Night at school?
- Did they make sure you did your homework, read with you, and ensure that you got enough sleep every night?
- Were you able to talk with them about difficulties you were having such as teasing by peers or difficulty learning math concepts?

- Are there things you wish you could have learned when you were a child or opportunities you wished you had been given?

If you feel your parents didn't provide you with the help you needed to succeed in school, why was that?

- Were they working two jobs while struggling to put food on the table for seven kids or were they out at the local bar getting drunk?
- Did they have learning difficulties that made it difficult for them to help you with your homework?
- Did they do the best they could, given the circumstances?
- Did your parents talk to you about politics or current events, teach you how to handle money or make home repairs, talk about their own educational experiences, or model lifelong learning by taking courses or going back to school as an adult?

Now think about your role as a parent.

- What would you like to teach your children?
- Do you spend time with your young children playing games, reading, doing puzzles, or visiting museums?
- Do you help your older children with their homework, talk with them about their difficulties in school, educate them about things like nutrition or how to budget money, and encourage them to follow their dreams?
- Do you advocate for your children when they have difficulty at school and help them get access to opportunities for learning?
- Are you a supportive parent or do you place too much pressure on your children to succeed?

Think about each of your children.

- What are their strengths?
- How can you help each of them to reach their potential and grow up to be compassionate, happy, and productive adults?

CHAPTER 9

EMOTIONS

Emotions are what make our children's personalities come alive and connect us to them at a deep and meaningful level. We experience great pleasure when we see our kids light up when we walk into the room or watch them giggle with excitement when we swim with them or push them on a swing. We work hard to make them happy by doing everything from working extra hours so they can attend camp with their friends to spending the weekend building them a swing set to create a lifetime of happy childhood memories.

Our emotions are often closely linked to theirs. When our children are happy, we usually feel happy, too. When they're heartbroken, we often feel incredibly sad ourselves. Sometimes, though, our children create different emotions in us than they're experiencing. For example, your teen may experience a thrill out of driving too fast, while his bad behavior leaves you feeling terrified. Your first grader may feel nervous about joining her peers at a party, but you may feel frustrated as you try to convince her she'll have a great time if she'll just go inside.

We try hard to protect our children from experiencing negative emotions, but it's not possible to do so nor is that a good idea. No matter what we do, there will be times when our children feel sad, anxious, angry, and frightened. At times they will envy their peers, feel guilt over things they've done or said, and regret choices they have made. We can work to prevent them from experiencing some negative emotions by trying to protect them from people who might harm them, remain in their lives after a divorce, or provide love and support when they experience a loss. We can make life easier for them by helping them secure the required skills to meet their needs and raising them in a loving and nurturing environment. The truth is, though, we can't protect our children from everything. Despite our best efforts, all of them will find themselves needing to cope with intense, negative events during their lives.

As parents, our job is to give them the gift of the best life possible by minimizing negative events, helping them learn how to verbally express their feelings, providing support and love, and helping them develop the skills they need to cope effectively with negative emotions.

Facts about Emotions

It's important to teach our children that emotional growth and development continues throughout life. We can teach this through modeling. We can say things to them such as, "I used to get angry when I had to wait in long lines, but I'm really trying to learn to be more patient" or "I have a hard time letting myself cry, but I'm trying to allow myself to cry more when I'm feeling really sad." Show them how we learn to cope as our lives change and as we face challenges such as coping with the death of family members, sending children off to college, handling a divorce, worrying about finances after losing a job, or making mistakes or bad choices.

One of the most difficult things children have to learn is how to modulate their emotions. They must learn it's okay to feel angry but not to act out their feelings in an aggressive rage. We need to help them understand sometimes they'll feel jealous of peers but that having those feelings doesn't give them the right to be mean or say hurtful things.

It can be difficult for people to learn these skills and some people never acquire them. Just drive down a crowded freeway, and you are likely to see at least one adult displaying road rage. Go to a bar, and you'll see more than one person using alcohol to minimize feelings such as sadness or social anxiety.

Children's ability to control their emotions depends on so many factors including whether or not they've developed the skills they need to cope effectively with their emotions, the maturity of their nervous system, the behavior of people in their environment, and their temperament. Even children who are usually good at controlling their emotions may struggle when they're experiencing intense stressors such as the death of a parent, lack of sleep, or illness.

Children need to learn how to identify their feelings. In order for children to learn how to control their emotions, they need to be able to articulate them verbally. This is far more difficult than it sounds. First, they need to learn how to discriminate between feelings. For example, they need to be able to know that when they feel one way it means they are angry, but a different feeling is called sadness. As a parent, help your child learn how to identify and label emotions. Be specific when talking about feelings. Ask your child if she feels angry, resentful, jealous, or frustrated instead of asking her if she's "upset." When your child is young, use terms like mad, sad, or frustrated. As she matures, begin to teach her how to identify more complex feelings such as resentment, shame, guilt, envy, or rejection.

Define the terms for your child and provide clear examples to help her understand what you're saying. You may find it would behoove you to learn more about feelings yourself. Perhaps it's difficult for you to distinguish between guilt and shame. We feel guilty when we do something we know we shouldn't have done; we feel shame when we think there's something bad about us we wouldn't want others to see. Emotions are so complicated, and many adults aren't able to label the full range of emotions. For instance, some people may become angry when in reality they're experiencing feelings such as rejection, envy, insecurity, or intense sadness.

Model identifying feelings by labeling your own feelings. For instance, you might say, "I'm so frustrated. I must have tried ten times to start the lawn mower, but I just couldn't get it to start" or "I felt so sad and rejected when the neighbors had a party and didn't invite your dad and me."

It's important to teach our children that negative emotions are a part of who we are and aren't necessarily bad. Explain to them that emotions communicate messages to us. For example, we realize how much a friend meant to us when we cry over his death or how important being accepted into college is when we worry about doing poorly on the SAT's.

Negative emotions can teach us so many things about ourselves. Explain to your child that experiencing a negative emotion can be a good thing. For example, fear of being in a car accident can prevent us from driving too fast, anger can motivate us to leave a relationship in which we aren't being treated kindly, and guilt can make us take responsibility for our actions.

Teach your children to trust their feelings. It's important to validate your children's feelings. Say things like, "You're so sad. You really loved Sam, didn't you?" instead of "Why are you crying? He was just a hamster." It may seem trivial, but it's not. How you respond when your child feels sad about the death of his hamster will impact how he will cope with other more devastating losses when he's older. If you tell him not to cry over the death of his pet, he may grow up to feel it isn't okay to cry about other deaths, even the loss of friends or relatives.

Teach your children to listen to that little voice inside of them and to trust their emotions. Tell them if they feel uncomfortable around someone, they should trust their feelings, avoid being alone with him or her, and explain their discomfort to you or another adult. Talk to children about listening to their conscience and not engaging in behaviors with peers if they feel those behaviors are wrong. Remind them you won't always be with them and that they'll need to trust their intuition in order to make the right decisions. Give them examples of how you use your intuition to make decisions. For example, tell them about the time your doctor thought you were fine, but you felt you weren't. You sought a second opinion and discovered you were right, something was wrong with you. Or when you felt uncomfortable when a sales person came to your door, and you decided not to let him into the house.

Emotions help us meet our needs. We all have numerous needs. We seek adventure to give ourselves stimulation, intimacy in order to feel close to others, learning to satisfy our curiosity, friendships because we're social animals who need to bond with others, and jobs so we can provide for our families. Our emotions help us meet these needs by motivating us to take action. When we feel bored, we seek stimulation. When we feel lonely, we look for opportunities to spend time with friends or family. When we feel scared, we look for someone to keep us safe. If we're worried about paying the bills, we apply for jobs.

Children may not always be conscious of the needs they are trying to meet and, instead, display behaviors that accomplish their goals. Unfortunately, sometimes we stop the behavior without finding a more appropriate way to help a child meet his needs. We may tell a child to sit quietly during Thanksgiving dinner when maybe a better solution would be to let Uncle Rick take him for a short walk before returning to the table. The child's need to get up and move around may be satisfied while also allowing the two of them to spend some quality uninterrupted time together (and give you a few minutes of time to enjoy your dinner).

It can be difficult for children to identify their needs, even when they're teens. Ask your kids how they feel and what would make them feel better. As they mature, work to keep the lines of communication open.

Temperament influences how children respond to emotions. Everyone, including children, feels emotions differently. Some people remain generally calm and don't necessarily feel intense emotions. Others experience minor stressors with more intensity and are quick to display signs of anger or frustration. There are some people who are often elated or may be naturally more dramatic. There are numerous differences in temperament, even in siblings.

We know that environmental factors also affect how a child responds to stimuli. A child who was always pretty even tempered and confident may become frightened easily after her house is damaged in a fire or she witnessed her parent being mugged. As parents we have to adapt our parenting to the specific needs of each child. We may need to encourage one child to socialize more and his sibling to work on controlling her anger.

Thoughts can affect emotions. As a student, I learned that there is nothing wrong with emotions, only how they're expressed. That is true, but there's more to it. That statement implies we can't control what we feel, only how we choose to express those feelings. Over time, however, I've learned we really can control or alter what emotions we experience. We do that by changing our thoughts. For example, if someone looks at us in a mean way, we can feel angry but choose to either not express it or to say something appropriate such as "Please don't look at me like that."

We can do more than that though. We can think about the situation and change our feelings. We can think of other possible reasons for his behavior. Maybe his stomach is hurting him and his mean look has nothing to do with us. Or we can ask ourselves if we may have inadvertently made him angry by accidentally cutting in front of him in line or not responding when he asked us a question we didn't hear.

We can help our children learn to look at their emotional reactions and to ask themselves if they're interpreting the situation correctly. Explain to an older sibling that his baby sister isn't trying to be mean when she takes his toy. We can tell him she just doesn't understand the toy is his and that she shouldn't take it. We can teach our children to no longer fear daddy long legs spiders by teaching them those spiders don't bite.

Different cultures respond differently to emotions.
Teach your children that various cultures express emotions differently and encourage them to be understanding of others. In one culture, people may be comfortable hugging casual friends, while people in another culture may maintain more distance and touch each other less frequently.

Funerals are one place where cultural differences are quite obvious. Some families protect children from death and rarely bring them to funerals, while others feel that children benefit from being able to attend funerals or visit dying relatives. In some families, people weep throughout the funeral, while in other families people are less expressive.

You and your spouse or partner will need to discuss how you want to bring up your children, especially if you were raised in different cultures. This can be difficult, but the important thing is to do what you feel is best for your child's emotional growth and development.

Let your children know it's okay to feel sad, angry, and afraid. Children come into this world expressing emotions openly. When they're sad, they cry. When something's funny, they laugh. Over time, though, we begin to teach them to control their emotions. That does have its advantages. For instance, children need to learn that someone may look funny, but it's not okay to laugh out loud at the person. They may think their teacher is nasty and strongly dislike her, but it's not a good idea to blurt that out in class.

Unfortunately, in an effort to teach children to express emotions appropriately, sometimes we give them the wrong message and tell them it isn't okay to feel emotions. For example, far too many men grew up hearing it isn't okay to cry. Many women were comforted when they cried but told it's wrong for them to show anger. Usually the message goes even further and children learn it isn't okay to feel certain emotions.

Some parents find it difficult to see their children feeling sad, angry, or frustrated and sometimes, for instance, a divorced parent may feel incredibly guilty because her son feels sad when his father leaves after each visit. She may become angry at her son when he cries because seeing his sadness makes her feel guilty.

Although it can be difficult to watch our children experience unpleasant emotions, we need to allow them to do so if they're going to grow up to be emotionally healthy adults. If your child does something bad and feels guilty, let her feel that. Those feelings will help her behave more appropriately in the future. You don't want to teach your child to not have a conscience. You also want to help your child learn how to tolerate feelings of loss, frustration, and jealousy. If she feels sad over the loss of a pet, refrain from running out the same day to buy a new one. Give her a chance to feel sad and to grieve. If your child is angry because you won't buy him everything he wants, let him get mad. It's better to have an occasionally angry child than to create a spoiled, self-centered adult. Try not to make the mistake we all make upon occasion. Don't buy your children things so they won't feel angry, sad, lonely, or guilty. It may work in the short term but is not a long-term solution.

Help your children to process their emotions. Teach them the importance of dealing with negative feelings in a productive way. Explain it can be harmful to their well being when they avoid feeling sad over a loss. They may experience headaches, have difficulty focusing, or feel sick. They may feel depressed or have trouble getting along with their peers. Help them to understand that by allowing themselves to mourn the loss, they help themselves feel better. If they feel the sadness and talk about those feelings, eventually they will feel happy again. Coping with negative feelings isn't easy, but people who are able to process their feelings are better able to cope with crises and continue to enjoy their lives despite the challenges they face.

Also let your children know it's okay to feel love. Most parents are more comfortable with the expression of positive emotions than negative ones, but that's not the case for all parents. If you grew up in a home where your parents never told you they loved you or didn't give you hugs and kisses, you may feel uncomfortable expressing love to your children. You'll need to remember that your family was dysfunctional and your own children need to be shown love. Don't worry. Over time you'll feel more comfortable expressing positive emotions.

If you were sexually abused as a child, you may not know the difference between appropriate expressions of love and sexual abuse. If you struggle with that issue, the best thing to do is to go to group therapy for sexual abuse survivors or individual therapy. Don't be afraid to ask questions or read books written for abuse survivors, particularly about maintaining appropriate boundaries.

Children respond to both verbal and nonverbal cues about their emotions. Sometimes we don't realize how tuned into emotions our children really are. You may tell your child you love her, but if you stiffen up when she gives you a hug, she'll question how much you really do love her. When you tell your son you aren't angry, he'll look at your face and body language and decide whether or not he thinks you're telling the truth.

So what do you do if you want to express one emotion verbally, but in truth you feel differently? I think the answer is you tell the truth. For example, if your son breaks a vase that has sentimental value and you know it was an accident, you might say, "I know you didn't mean to break it. I forgive you. I'm not blaming you, but I am mad that it's broken."

Another example: "I know I don't seem happy about the award you won, but that's because I have a terrible headache. It doesn't mean I'm not happy for you and proud of you. Let me lay down for a while, and when I get up I want to hear all about your award."

Learn to identify signs of depression. Everyone has times when they feel sad or depressed, but be careful not to mistake depression and suicidal feelings for typical teenage moodiness. The teen years are particularly challenging for kids and some do go through times when they become clinically depressed and even suicidal. Often kids become very sad when they're depressed. They might cry easily, become withdrawn, give things away, talk about death, sleep too much or too little, and gain or lose weight.

Other kids, particularly the younger ones, may respond differently. They may act out aggressively, argue a lot, or become angry for no apparent reason. Take any major change in behavior seriously and don't be afraid to seek help from mental health professionals. Ask the child's friends and teachers if they've noticed a change or are also concerned. Don't forget to watch for signs of alcohol or drug use. Some teens become depressed when using substances or use them to self-medicate feelings of depression.

Medications can be helpful but are not always the answer. Some children experience intense emotions and benefit from psychotropic medication. I'm not opposed to the use of psychotropic medications and know they can be helpful, but they aren't the answer to all emotional problems. For instance, a child who is very depressed and having difficulty functioning or is at risk for suicide is likely to benefit from an antidepressant. One with intense anxiety may be better able to socialize with peers and participate in age-appropriate activities when he's on an anti-anxiety medication for a short period of time.

Medication usually works best when combined with psychotherapy and isn't the answer in all situations. It's important to remember there's no magic pill to protect us from feeling intense emotions. A child who loses a parent may benefit from medication initially to cope with the crisis but will still need to grieve the loss. An anxious child may function better on medication, but the best solution may be to address conflict in the home through marital or family therapy.

Kids sometimes use self-destructive behaviors to cope with intense emotions. Adolescence can be a very stressful time for kids and sometimes the emotions are more than they can tolerate. They may try to relieve the intense feelings by engaging in behaviors such as cutting or burning themselves. Usually these behaviors are associated with intense feelings, but sometimes teens engage in them in order to be accepted by a peer group. Regardless of the reason, parents should take their children to a therapist if they're engaging in this type of behavior.

Everyone needs to accept that they sometimes experience negative emotions. Teach your children that, although you think they're wonderful people, sometimes they will think thoughts that aren't kind or experience feelings they don't like. Say things to your child such as, "There are a lot of things I really like about myself but some things I don't like. I don't like the fact I felt jealous when the neighbors won the lottery and I didn't" or "I don't like that I get mad if I can't have things my way.

It's not right, and I need to change that about myself, but I'd be lying if I said I don't feel that way sometimes."

Explain to your children that, although everyone occasionally has unkind thoughts, it's important not to act on those thoughts. Teach your children the first step to becoming kinder people is to admit to themselves they have both positive and negative aspects of themselves.

Help your child learn effective coping strategies. Children begin learning how to tolerate negative feelings when they are infants. We comfort them when they're distraught, nurture them, and reassure them we will always be there for them when they need us. This is important because we know that children who form a secure attachment to their parents are better able to cope with the stressors they'll face in life.

So how do you help your child feel safe and secure? You hug her when she's sad, encourage her to tell you how she feels, and validate her feelings. You need to be dependable, nurturing, and let her know you always love her, even when you don't like her behavior.

Your child can learn how to cope with her emotions by observation as you model effective strategies such as talking about feelings, going for a walk, doing yoga, practicing relaxation techniques, listening to music, or taking time to relax.

Teach your child how to integrate feelings. In order to become emotionally healthy adults, children need to learn to integrate their feelings. In other words, they need to be able to feel more than one feeling at a time. If your son is able to integrate his feelings, he may feel angry with you for taking the car keys away from him, but he knows, despite his anger, he still loves you.

You can use modeling to teach your children how to integrate their emotions. You could say, "I felt scared standing up and speaking at the reception but, at the same time, I was proud of myself for being able to do so" or "I know you're angry because I won't let you go to the party, but I wonder if you're also feeling a little relieved knowing you might feel pressured by the others to drink."

Teach compassion and empathy. As your children grow older, it's important for them to learn from you to think about how other people feel. The best way to do this is by treating them with compassion and showing them you genuinely care about how they feel. They, in turn, will treat others the same way.

Questions to Ponder

Take a few minutes and think about yourself and your emotions.

- Can you express your feelings easily? If not, why is that?
- Are you uncomfortable letting people see you cry, do you worry you'll lose control if you allow yourself to get angry, or do you feel too vulnerable when you let people know how you're feeling?
- How did your family respond to your feelings? When you cried after skinning your knee, did your mother pick you up, give you a hug, and tell you everything would be okay or did she ignore your cries for help or tell you to stop crying?
- Did people talk about feelings in your family? For instance, did people tell each other when they were angry or did they pretend they weren't, but then act out in a passive-aggressive manner?

Now think about your children.

- How do you respond to your children when they're sad, angry, or scared? Do you comfort them like you should or is this something you need to work on?

- How do you respond when they are sad or scared and how do their feelings make you feel?
- Do you feel comfortable talking to your children about emotions? Do you feel you can help them learn to modulate their affect and express their feelings with words or do you need help with this?
- Are you able to let your children experience negative emotions when that would be beneficial?
- Are you able to help them mourn losses?
- Do you let them feel guilty when they've done something wrong or do you allow them to blame their inappropriate behavior on somebody else?

Set aside some time today to notice the range of emotions your children experience and the ways they express them. Notice how each child experiences things differently and how their emotional experiences make each of them interesting and unique.

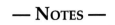

— NOTES —

Chapter 10

Relationships

When we decide to have a child, what is it we really want? I think, for most parents, there's only one answer. We're looking for a wonderful relationship that will last forever. Before we have our first child, we daydream about the time we'll spend with her. We picture ourselves rocking our newborn to sleep in our arms, playing with our toddler for hours, reading to our young child as we tuck her into bed and tell her we love her, and helping our teenager cope with the many challenges she will face in life. We want her to love us, and we hope to give her the skills she'll need to form wonderful relationships with friends and eventually with her spouse and her own children.

We all know the relationship we develop with our children will enrich our lives and will serve as the basis for all of their future relationships. The quality of the parent-child relationship will help determine if our children will follow their teachers' directions, feel confident to stay overnight at a friend's house, be able to form friendships with peers, and develop a healthy, intimate relationship with a lover when they grow up. We will strive to do our best to form a close, loving relationship with our child, but it's perfectly normal for us to wonder if we'll be "good enough" parents. We can pretend to be confident that we'll do a great job of parenting, but I think most of us would be lying if we said we didn't have times when we worried our efforts might not be good enough.

Let's face it. Being a parent is not an easy job. It's difficult to raise children, and they often trigger feelings in us that are more intense than we could have ever imagined before we became parents. We are terrified the first time our baby spikes a high fever or we watch our child cross the street on his own. We'd like to think it gets easier over time, but we know it doesn't. We worry when our teen goes on a first date, passes her driver's test and borrows the car, or forgets to call to say she'll be home late. We feel intense sadness when our child cries when his friend moves away, his girlfriend breaks up with him, or he heads off to college and leaves us with an empty nest.

Relationships with our children are challenging, even if we have wonderful kids and are doing a great job parenting them. The parent-child relationship, like all relationships, is not without conflict. Children test limits, argue with us, and have times when they push us away. They can make us feel like we're on an emotional roller coaster, especially during the toddler and teen years. One day our children will light up when they see us and can't wait to tell us endless details about their lives, while the next day they may close us out and tell us to mind our own business. In the morning they may remind us they love us and in the afternoon tell us they wish they had different "nicer" parents. The parent-child relationship is far from easy, but most parents wouldn't trade it for the world.

So how do we have a great relationship with our children and help them to be able to form healthy relationships with people both within and outside of the family?

Facts about Relationships

The parent-child relationship is the most important relationship you'll ever have. I don't think parents realize how much they're going to love their children until they have them. I know I didn't. Before we have our children, we hear parents say that they'd die in a second if it meant saving their child's life, but most of us do not understand how true that statement is until we bond with our own children.

The parent-child relationship is very powerful and is the most effective tool for molding children into loving, wonderful people. Unfortunately, if used improperly, the relationship can damage our children as easily as it can help them grow. If we do a great job, our children will likely become successful, form healthy relationships, and be happy. If we fail, though, the consequences can be devastating. No one wants to raise a child who can't hold a job, feels unable to end an abusive marriage, becomes addicted to drugs or alcohol, commits crimes, or feels unhappy.

The pressure to succeed as a parent is great, but I believe anyone can become a good parent, even people who were raised in dysfunctional families or by incompetent parents. Some people will find the task more challenging and need more support to succeed, but everyone can help their children to become happy, emotionally healthy adults.

Bonding with a child takes time. The parent-child relationship grows with time. When you first see your baby, you'll feel intense feelings of love, but over time you will develop a closer relationship with him. Your bond with your child will intensify as you allow yourself to feel closer to him, he begins to maintain eye contact with you, smiles back at you, stops crying the moment you pick him up, snuggles with you, reaches for you to pick him up, and eventually calls your name.

You and your spouse need time to bond with your child. It's nice to have help, especially when you're exhausted after giving birth, but make sure the people who are helping you respect your need to have quality alone time with your newborn. You will build your relationship with your child when you give her a bath, feed her, and sit in a quiet room rocking her to sleep. Avoid the temptation to have a relative or nanny take over these important tasks on a regular basis. The time spent completing the everyday tasks in life together are what really form the foundation of quality relationships.

Make sure you allow your child's other parent to share in these activities. Years ago, mothers bathed their kids, bandaged their skinned knees, and cheered them on at the little league games while fathers went to work. Today, we know children do best when they can form close relationships with both parents. Mothers tend to feel more comfortable with new babies than the fathers do. Many of us cared for younger siblings or baby-sat throughout junior and senior high school. Men perhaps didn't have those opportunities and may be uncomfortable holding their new babies. They may need suggestions on how to comfort a crying baby, opportunities to become more comfortable caring for an infant, and encouragement as they struggle to bond with their children. Sometimes mothers are tempted to jump in and calm a fussy infant, but it's important to step back and give their baby's father a chance to learn new skills and feel comfortable in his new role.

You may experience negative emotions as you begin to bond with your infant. The parent-child relationship is very intense and may cause you to feel angry, scared, or sad. Infants are extremely dependent, especially on their mothers. Many want to be held every second they're awake and their needs often seem endless. Some mothers, but not all, love this. People who aren't comfortable with dependency may feel suffocated by having a baby attached to her breast for hours every day. She may wish she could just give herself some personal space. People whose needs weren't met by their own parents may feel angry or sad when they see how much their children need, and they may wonder why their parents didn't meet their own needs.

If your baby's dependency makes you feel uncomfortable, relax and see if those feelings begin to subside as you bond with your child. Don't withdraw from your child, but occasionally ask your spouse to watch the baby so you can take a drive alone in the car or go out to lunch with a friend in order to have a break. Seek professional help if the unpleasant feelings intensify rather than subside over time or you feel they're interfering with your ability to form a close relationship with your child.

The parent-child relationship is like no other relationship you will ever have. When we bond with our children, we begin to instinctively experience emotions we don't feel, or feel less intensely, in other relationships. We may find strength we never knew we had when it comes to protecting our children from harm. We may never have imagined we would make huge sacrifices in order to meet our children's needs.

Help your children develop a wide range of relationships. Relationships play a major role in everyone's life. We have friends, relatives, acquaintances, co-workers, lovers, bosses, etc. and know that relationships can be complex. Give your kids opportunities to play with peers in structured and unstructured activities and form close friendships with adults.

Being a good parent means placing your children's needs before you own. Why do some parents have a hard time placing the needs of their children before their own? There are many reasons. Perhaps the primary reason, though, is it can be difficult to meet the needs of others if your own needs were never met. That's not to say that people who were deprived as children can't become great parents. They can, but they may need to attend parenting classes, make an effort to read some parenting books, or go to therapy to address their own issues in order to become a better parent.

Some people aren't good parents because they're too self-centered. The reality is kids cost money, lots of money. If you don't want to spend money on someone else, perhaps you shouldn't be a parent. If you're married to or living with someone who becomes angry about having to pay for diapers, buy baby food, or spend time with the child, encourage him or her to go with you to couples counseling. If it looks like change is not going to occur, think about the environment you're providing for your child and whether or not you should remove your child from it.

The parent-child relationship sets the tone for all future relationships. Your children will have great difficulty having healthy relationships as adults if you are cold, rejecting, cruel, abusive, demeaning, or unavailable. That's not to say that people who have parents who treat them in that manner can't have wonderful relationships as adults, but first they will have to resolve their issues in order to do so.

For instance, if you are harsh and controlling, your child may have great difficulty interacting with authority figures such as a boss or a teacher. If you come in and out of your child's life, she's likely to push people away out of a fear they will leave her. Or she may remain in an abusive relationship because she can't tolerate the thought of being alone. If you cheat on your spouse, she's likely to behave the same way when she grows up. Does that mean you need to be perfect? No, of course not.

You can make mistakes, but above all you need to treat your child with kindness. Some mistakes will not cause damage, especially if you take responsibility for your behavior, apologize to your child, and behave more appropriately in the future. But some behaviors will cause severe emotional damage to your children, and there are lines you decide upon that you will never cross no matter how angry you feel.

Treat your children like you would want to be treated. It can be difficult to know how to parent, especially if your parents weren't nurturing parents. Probably the easiest way to decide how to interact with your children is to keep two things in mind: ask yourself "how would I want to be treated in this situation" and "what message am I giving them?" For example, if you did something wrong, would you want someone to scream at you, hit you, or demean you or would you want them to help you learn to behave more appropriately in the future? If you ignore your child, are you making him feel unloved or giving him the message there's something about him you don't like?

Make sure you are never cruel, abusive, or neglectful towards your children. Those are lines you can never cross. It's your responsibility to meet your child's physical and emotional needs even when you have needs of your own. Never tell him you hate him or that he's ugly, stupid, or that you wish you never had him. Do not deprive him of necessary health care, an education, or the opportunity to bond with you. If you find yourself crossing these lines, do the right thing and seek professional help immediately.

Remember that you're the parent, not a friend. We've all heard this a million times, but it can't be said too much. All of us want our children to like us. But being a good parent means sometimes they won't like us. When we're telling them "no" or refusing to give them something they're sure they absolutely need and deserve, they may react negatively toward us. But that's okay. In order to help our children grow up to be nice people, we have to set limits and at times say "no" to them.

Why is it some parents interact with their children more like a peer rather than a parent? There are many different reasons. Some parents don't have enough friends of their own and hope their children will fill that void. Others are terrified of losing their children's love and will do anything to prevent their children from rejecting them.

When our kids dislike us, it's not always a bad thing. They may get angry with us at the time, but when they grow up they'll be glad we behaved as a parent and were willing to stand our ground to do what was best for them.

As a parent, there are many activities you can do with adults, but not with your kids. It's not okay to share alcohol with your teen so he'll let you hang out with him and his friends. It's also not okay to allow him to skip school so he'll think you're cool or let him stay up and not do his homework so he won't become angry with you.

Unfortunately, some parents don't set limits because they lack assertiveness skills or are afraid to make their children angry. No one enjoys dealing with an angry kid, but there is no way you can be a good parent without making your children angry on occasion. Parenting has its rewards, but it also comes with a great deal of responsibility. When you choose to be a parent, you need to do the hard work required to help create a wonderful person.

Model handling conflicts appropriately. Many people never reach their goals in life, can't seem to find happiness, or fail to maintain quality relationships because they have difficulty resolving conflicts. The fact is no matter how hard you try, you can't have a conflict-free relationship.

The best way to teach your children how to resolve conflicts is to model desirable behavior when you and your children have a conflict. When you disagree, respect their opinions and refrain from making nasty remarks or being accusatory. Instead, talk about how you feel and give them opportunities to express their feelings, show them that, when it's appropriate, you're willing to compromise and explain to them that you expect them to do the same. Let them know you always love them even when you're angry with them or don't like their behavior.

Be willing to take a good look at yourself and to admit when you're at fault. If your child is angry because he feels you always blame him for conflicts with his siblings, ask yourself if it's possible you might be doing just that. If you are, apologize to your child, thank him for talking to you about the issue, and change your behavior.

Sometimes parents assume they're always right and the child is always the one at fault, but that's not necessarily the case. We're not just parents; we're also people with our own issues, skill deficits, and problems. We need to show our children we take responsibility for our behavior and that we all spend a lifetime working at becoming better people.

Encourage your kids to talk about relationship problems. Relationships are difficult. Many adults have relationship issues, so you can imagine how challenging it is for pre-teens to handle hormones, teasing from peers, and competition with friends for attention from both same sex and opposite sex peers, not to mention problems with the numerous authority figures in their lives. Keep the lines of communication open and recognize that sometimes you'll have to intervene. Provide support, validate their feelings, and remind them that things usually get easier as they get older.

Don't underestimate the impact sibling relationships have on a child. Parents used to stay out of sibling conflicts, often attributing problems solely to sibling rivalry. It's true there are many times when we need to watch from the sidelines and give our children opportunities to work out things on their own. But sometimes we have to intervene in order to protect one child from being emotionally, physically, and perhaps even sexually abused by a sibling. We'd like to think our children won't hurt each other, but many therapists have heard story after story from adults who suffered years of abuse from siblings when they were growing up. Far too often they asked their parents for help but never received it.

Let all of your children know they can come to you for help if their sibling is hurting them. Tell them that while you will tolerate minor teasing, occasional arguments, and some yelling and anger, you won't tolerate cruelty, ongoing harassment, or abuse.

Let your children know that each of them is different and you love the fact they're all individuals with their own strengths and weaknesses. Make a conscious effort to nurture and facilitate their relationships with each other. Remember, you will not be there for your children forever. If you help them form close sibling relationships, they will have someone there for them long after you and your spouse are gone.

Make sure your relationship with your child is multi-dimensional. It's important to be a parent, not a friend, but that doesn't mean your relationship has to be built solely on ensuring that your child develops good values, follows rules, and respects authority. Your child also needs to have a relationship with you as a person. Have fun together. Go to the movies, tell jokes, ride bikes together, or go out to dinner so you can have time to talk without interruptions.

The relationship also needs to be two sided. As a parent, you need to maintain boundaries but share things about yourself so your child can get to know you better. When your son is learning to ride a bike, talk with him about your experiences when you got your first bike. When you move, tell your daughter about the time when you moved as a child and worried that you wouldn't be able to make friends. As your son applies to college, talk about the career decisions you made, the fun you had at college, and how you became the person you are today.

How do you know what information you should share and what you should keep to yourself? Consider the age of the child and the impact the information will have on him. A college-age child may be fine knowing you dated several women before you fell in love with his mother, but a young child is likely to find that fact disturbing. Even a college-age child, however, will not be comfortable hearing about your sexual encounters and shouldn't hear you glamorizing illegal, unethical, or nasty behavior.

When you answer questions, respond in a way that's helpful, not harmful. For example, if your child asks you if you ever got drunk in college, you might say, "Yes, but I wish I drank more responsibly. One time I got drunk, had a hangover, didn't show up at my internship, and was let go. I really regret that. I can't believe how stupid I was."

Maintain appropriate boundaries in your family. One problem many people have in relationships is difficulty maintaining good boundaries. If you don't maintain appropriate boundaries in your home, your children are unlikely to maintain them outside of the home. Maintaining boundaries is such a broad topic. It includes everything from not interrupting someone when they're speaking, not listening in on other people's conversations, closing doors when dressing or going to the bathroom, and not discussing your sex life with your children.

It's important to have clear boundaries and to be consistent in maintaining them. As your children grow older, you'll need to change the boundaries. For example, when your child was young you may have told him that how much you earn is not something you will discuss with him. But you may decide to talk about finances once he starts working, is looking at careers, and is applying to colleges.

Give your children the skills they need to form relationships. Relationships are so complex and many people spend their whole lives trying to learn how to develop and maintain healthy relationships with others. Your children are going to need to learn many relationship skills throughout their childhoods, and you will have the primary role in teaching them these skills. Explain things to them such as why we don't interrupt others when they're talking or the importance of listening and not monopolizing a conversation. Teach them to treat people with respect and insist that others treat them the same way. Show them how a good relationship works by forming a close and healthy relationship with them.

It's important to provide consequences when they're behaving inappropriately in relationships. For example, you may need to limit your child's use of the Internet if he posts hurtful remarks about his peers or insist that an adult be home whenever he invites friends over after learning he had a party at your house when you were out of town.

Learn about social networking sites. Kids now have large social networks on the Internet and maintain relationships with peers via the computer. Don't ban your children from connecting with peers on the Internet, but make sure you educate them about ways to keep themselves safe. Fortunately, schools teach children to be careful not to post identifying information such as their address or phone number and to restrict their site so that only approved friends can access it.

Provide opportunities for your children to spend time with peers. The Internet allows children to stay in touch with friends they met at camp years earlier or to interact with peers they may not ordinarily invite to their home or call on the phone but will chat with for hours on a social networking site. That's great, but communicating through writing is not the same as interacting with someone in person.

Teens need to be able to dance with their peers at the high school dance, interact with teammates on the sports team, work well with others on a classroom project, and have fun hanging out with friends. It's a huge leap from talking about music videos on a social networking site to asking a girl out, dancing with her, spending hours together on dates, and maintaining a teenage romance.

Encourage teens to join teams or clubs, attend school activities such as dances or field trips and invite friends to your home. Make sure you have items in your home that encourage play such as age-appropriate games or sports equipment.

Many structured activities for kids such as sports and camps insist the kids put away their cell phones and interact with their peers. When your child is spending time with friends, ask him to turn off his cell phone and, as a courtesy, not text other kids. Many children don't realize it's rude to text one friend while talking to another.

Educate your children about what behaviors are and are not acceptable in relationships. Today relationships are more complicated than ever. Kids become close friends on-line with peers who in the past they would have known only as casual acquaintances. Reality television gives teens the opportunity to watch the everyday lives of all kinds of people, many with values you may not endorse. I was shocked one afternoon when I walked past the TV and heard the couple on the show talking about planning to have sex under the covers in the next few minutes. That was the last thing I wanted my thirteen-year-old daughter to see.

Our kids are getting so many mixed messages today about relationships. We can tell them that people should have sex only when they're emotionally mature and in a committed relationship, but sometimes the media sends the message that cool kids have one-night stands with people they don't even know.

So how do we encourage our children to listen to us and not the media? Have open communication. For example, you can explain that you realize most people don't necessarily wait until marriage to have sex, but you do want them to wait until they're older. Empha-

^ize the need to form a mature relationship with some-one they genuinely love. Point out that if they become pregnant and have children when they're still children themselves, they certainly won't be ready to raise and support a family.

Teach your children they deserve to be treated with respect. Start teaching children about appropriate be-havior when they're just toddlers. Explain to them it's not okay to hit and make sure you model appropriate behavior. You can't tell your child not to hit someone and then hit your spouse. Many parents believe in spanking, but I think it's hard to explain to your child that hitting isn't okay and then to turn around and hit him a few hours later.

Show your kids how to treat people with kindness. Be polite by not interrupting people when they're talk-ing, listen attentively and ask questions during conver-sations, and be dependable and trustworthy. Explain to your children that good friends are kind and don't mistreat other people.

Years ago, children were taught to respect their elders no matter what. The message is different today. We want our children to show respect for adults, if those adults treat them kindly. Show your child that you won't allow people to hurt him. If you witness your son's guitar teacher being verbally abusive towards him, hire a new teacher and tell him you won't allow people to talk to him in that manner. If your daughter's peers are bullying her, show her that you will work with school personnel to put a stop to it. Teach children they should not remain in relationships that are toxic or where they're treated unkindly.

Consider buying a pet for your kids. Pets provide unconditional love and are great for teaching kids to be kind and caring.

Before buying a pet, however, you need to make sure it's the right decision for you and your family. For instance, before buying a dog consider whether you have the time and patience to walk a dog, if you can tolerate dog hair or muddy footprints on the carpet and if your children are old enough to help with the care and able to interact with him without pulling his tail or taking his toys away. Consider whether or not you can afford food and vet bills and can handle adding more responsibility to your already hectic life.

If you buy a pet, ask the sales clerk or a local vet what type of pet is best for you and your family. Let your child help select the pet and encourage her to bond with it. Show her how to treat the pet with kindness and have her participate in caring for it. Young children may be able to help brush him or pour the food in his bowl while older kids can be expected to feed and walk the pet every day.

Your relationship with your child will constantly change. I don't think we're ever quite prepared for changes in our relationships with our children. All you can do is enjoy it as it is in the moment and be flexible and willing to adapt when your child matures and suddenly wants to change the relationship. When your child wants to curl up in your lap and watch TV with you every night, enjoy it because the next day she may decide she's too old for that and never again sit on your lap. That sounds depressing, but I don't mean for it to be. As you lose one type of relationship with your child, you quickly gain another more mature type. Your child who no longer wants to sit on your lap may suddenly want to spend hours talking with you about the crush she has on the boy who sits in front of her at school. Or she may decide she wants to go on nightly bike rides with you.

Unfortunately, though, if you do a good job as a parent, your child will spend more time with peers and less time with you and then eventually leave the nest. You'll need to mourn the loss and learn to form a more mature, adult relationship with him. At each point of change in the relationship, there will be both losses and gains. Your child, who no longer raises his arms to be picked up, will be able to get in and out of the car on his own, making your life a little easier. He won't wrap his arms tightly around your neck and give you lots of kisses, but he may light up when you pick him up at camp or he spots you in the stands at his football game.

As your children change, there are some messages you want to give them. Let them know you won't hold them back, you are proud of the changes they're making, and that you'll be there for them when they make mistakes. Assure them you want them to gain independence and live their lives for themselves, not for you and, no matter what, you always love them.

Questions to Ponder

Think about your relationship with your parents.
- Were you close to them or did you find them to be detached, abusive, or unreliable?
- How did your relationship with your parents change as you grew older and how did your perspective change?
- For example, did you hate the fact they wouldn't let you attend parties when adults weren't present, but now, looking back, are glad they did that?

Think about your current relationships.
- Do you tend to have relationship issues?
- Do you need to learn more skills such as how to be

assertive, less controlling, or more willing to compromise in arguments?

- How do you feel about caring for a totally dependent infant? Does the dependency make you feel needed or leave you feeling suffocated and wishing you could have more personal space?

We all bring our own personal issues into raising our children.

- Do you get upset if you feel you're being rejected or angry when you feel you're losing control?
- Do you say things you shouldn't when you are angry or withdraw when your feelings have been hurt?
- What issues do you need to keep in check in order to do a good job parenting your children?
- How do you handle conflict? It's likely you will treat your child the same way you treat your spouse when you're angry.
- Can you resolve conflicts in a constructive way, or do you get nasty or make the situation worse?
- When you do make a mistake, do you apologize, take responsibility for actions or words, and change your behavior in the future?
- How do you handle change and separation?
- Are you emotionally prepared to help your children grow up and separate from you? Or are you concerned you might try to keep them dependent in order to meet your own needs?
- Do you allow yourself to enjoy your relationship with your children?
- Do you keep in mind that they will be grown up before you know it and work hard to minimize any regrets you might have about your parenting?
- Do you realize parenting is difficult? There will be conflicts and you will make mistakes, but chances are good you'll be a "good enough" parent.

Chapter 11

Happiness

We want our children to be happy. We know they won't feel that way all the time, but I think we'd all agree that we hope our children will look back on their childhoods and describe them as "happy."

When we think about children, we picture a child laughing when he's swinging, giggling as he runs through the sprinkler, or smiling from ear to ear as he opens presents at his birthday party. When we talk with friends about childhood, we reminisce about the fun we had or the things we wish had been different so we would have enjoyed our childhoods more.

We know all kinds of things made us happy when we were kids. Sometimes they were special occasions like a trip to Disney World, getting our first puppy, or the time our team won a state championship. If we think about it long enough, we're sure to remember many little things that gave us pleasure like the time we spent with a favorite aunt who always told interesting stories, the smile on our favorite teacher's face every time we walked into the classroom, or the fun we had baking cookies with our grandmother or riding on our grandfather's lawn tractor.

Unfortunately, some parents had tough childhoods and don't have many happy memories. They may have spent far too much time doing chores and not enough time playing, or they may have lived stressful lives in homes where people were abusive, neglectful, depressed, alcoholic, or violent. Some of them will find it difficult to give their kids a better life than they had, but most will be able to do so.

How do you give your children a childhood that will bring them a lifetime of happy memories?

Let your child show you how to be happy. Children are naturally happy. They laugh at silly things and don't care if anyone else thinks they're funny. They find pleasure in the simple things of life such as watching a bee pollinate a flower, splashing in a mud puddle, sitting together to read a book, or racing their siblings to the tree in the backyard. They take the time to satisfy their senses by doing everything from smelling a rose or swinging on a tire swing to making music with pots and pans or watching waves smashing on the rocks at the beach.

I love to go on vacations with my kids. They force me to have fun that I don't think I'd have if they weren't so insistent. They demand we go on family bike rides, walk along the beach together, go down slides at water parks, ride on a tube behind a motorboat, or spend the day at an amusement park.

Facts about Happiness

Don't assume you know what's best when it comes to having fun with your kids. Sure, you probably have some great ideas, but if you ask your kids for suggestions, their ideas are probably even better.

Avoid bringing your children down. We all have times when we're stressed or unhappy, but be careful not to burden your children with your feelings. Growing up with a depressed parent can be very harmful to children. If you are depressed, suffer from a chronic illness, or are experiencing a great deal of stress, work hard to ensure that your child has times with you when you're pleasant and happy. You may need to go to a therapist or support group or take medication if your depression is severe. Make a decision to keep negative comments to yourself during the special time you spend with your child and try to find ways to brighten her day.

When my kids were little, my husband had severe Lyme disease. Despite the fact he had been sick in bed for a week, we took a family trip to the school so the kids could play on the swings. He made sure not to complain about his exhaustion and to smile and talk with the kids as they played on the equipment. They had a great time and seemed happy to see him doing better. That activity was good for the kids and also for my husband. Even though he felt sick, he decided we should stop for ice cream on the way home. He had been reluctant to get out of bed that day, but he felt so much better once he spent some time with the kids.

Give your children opportunities to explore the world. Kids love to see new places and experience new things. It's great if you can afford to send your children on international trips or camps where they can experience everything from horseback riding or volunteering in South America or swimming with dolphins in Florida. But even without money, you can still help your children see the world. They can apply for scholarships to pay for international programs, read books about far-away lands, check out travel videos from the library, study nature at the local conservation center, or welcome an exchange student into your home. Take your children to volunteer at the local soup kitchen, attend the free classical piano concert at a local college, or go to the pet shop to look at the different breeds of fish, dogs, birds, and rodents.

Let your children play. Life isn't all about work. Play is just as important to their growth and development as studying is. People who succeed in today's world are the ones who can think outside of the box. They don't learn how to do that by spending every minute in classes and structured activities. They develop that ability by playing, using their imaginations, and being creative.

Adults who are truly happy know how to have fun and continue to play throughout their lives. When I was a kid, we rarely saw adults riding bikes, skating, or playing sports, but fortunately things have changed. Be a good role model for your kids and go outside and play. Join a neighborhood adult basketball team, buy that horse you always wanted, jump on your kids' trampoline, or play a game of capture the flag with your kids.

Spend time with your children. All the money in the world won't buy your children happiness. Kids are happy when they have parents who make them a priority. They love to be surprised when Mom cuts her business trip short to show up at their baseball game or Dad insists on going to school to read a book to his daughter's first grade class. Infants love it when their parents hold, rock, or sing to them.

Young children want nothing more than for Mom or Dad to serve as a playmate or to hold them on their lap during family movie night. Teens do want more time alone but feel lost if their parents don't remind them they're always on their minds. Comments like, "When I was at the mall, I saw a shirt you might like. Do you want to go back and look at it with me?" or "We watched a movie last night when you were sleeping over at Kate's house. We were sure you would have loved it. Do you want to watch movies with us next weekend?" Remarks like these go a long way in reminding them they are always loved even as they begin to grow up and develop more of a life outside of the family.

Give your kids a positive view of the world. Be optimistic. Give them a sense of hope. The world is a stressful place these days and kids don't need to be burdened with life's problems.

Happy people tend to see the glass as half full, not half empty. Teach your children how to see that half-full glass. For example, if your son's best friend isn't in his new third grade class, don't say, "You're really going to miss him. I wish that hadn't happened." Instead say something like, "You'll be able to spend time with him after school, like you always have, but now you can make new friends, too." Refrain from being invalidating or preventing your child from talking about sad topics. Help him learn how to look for the positive aspects of situations. Some parents are really good at this, but some, especially depressed parents, can struggle to find good aspects of bad situations.

Let your child decide what makes him happy. Happiness means something different for all of us. Some people get great pleasure from collecting model airplanes, walking on the beach, or spending time with friends, while other people enjoy reading books alone, studying mathematics, or listening to music. Encourage your children to find their own path to happiness. Give them opportunities to try different things and to develop the skills they need to be successful at what they do.

Your definition of happiness probably includes having children or you wouldn't be reading this book. However, your child may be happier someday in a childless marriage or living a single's life filled with time for her career and travel plans. You may enjoy spending time in your place of worship, while your child may feel spiritually fulfilled when he helps children in an underdeveloped nation or serves food at a shelter.

Encourage your children to dream. It's important for us to make decisions, especially financial ones, that are based in reality, but it's okay to fantasize sometimes, too. Fantasy is fun. That's why we attend movies, travel to Disney World, and buy lottery tickets. It's why our little girls dress up in princess dresses and our sons swear they'll be able to fly like a superhero when they grow a little bigger.

Dreaming gives us goals to work towards and is a coping strategy that often works very well and provides hours of fun. After all, what kid hasn't spent many a boring class daydreaming? We live only once and a few moments or hours spent thinking magical thoughts never hurt anyone.

Let them win. We're all happy when we succeed. We love to win and so do our kids. Kids love to have their art work picked to decorate the school corridor, earn the perfect attendance award, have a role in the school play, be on the baseball team that wins the state finals, or win the French award at eighth grade graduation. Give your children opportunities to win by encouraging them to take risks and compete. If they lose, point out to them that losing will only make winning someday that much more meaningful.

Everyone can win at something. Recently a child with a disability in my daughter's high school class was thrilled when she earned a place on the junior varsity cheerleading squad. What an exciting start to high school for a girl who has worked so hard to fit in with her peers. I was thrilled to hear that her peers were genuinely happy for her.

Make a big deal out of your children's successes. Put the trophy on the mantle, hang the certificate of achievement in a prominent place in your home, or make a scrapbook for newspaper articles about your daughter's success in sports. Remember that winning doesn't have to mean beating out top contestants. A winner is someone who beats her own time on the track or climbs back up on the balance beam after a fall and finishes her routine. A winner is someone who forfeits a race because she stops to help an injured peer reach the finish line or gets her picture hung up on the "Most Improved Student" wall at school.

My daughter worked hard to learn how to play polo. After two years of training for this difficult equestrian sport, she was selected as the alternate for the high school polo team at a local college. She was thrilled and was happier with that accomplishment than her easily earned academic successes. I quickly posted the news on my facebook page so she could see how proud I am of her hard-earned accomplishment.

Meet your children's needs. One simple way to make your children happy is to meet their needs. If they've been outside sledding, welcome them back into the house with a warm fire in the fireplace, a cup of hot chocolate, and freshly baked cookies. If your son is sad because none of his friends can come over to play, drop what you're doing and spend an hour playing a board game or reading a book with him. If your child is climbing the walls from boredom, go for a walk or shoot baskets with him.

Give your kids lots of opportunities to talk. Talking is great for making people happy. When your daughter is sad, let her talk, cry, and talk some more. Listen quietly and let her know you truly care about how she feels. When your son is anxious about starting kindergarten, encourage him to talk with you about what he thinks it will be like and what worries him most. Reassure him that he will have a kind and supportive teacher, will make new friends, and can count on you to be waiting for him when he gets off the bus.

Kids go through so many changes during childhood, and they love to talk about them. It makes them happy to tell their parents every detail of their day at school or the plot in the latest book they are reading. Toddlers and young children love to ask questions. I know that can be tiresome when it goes on for too long, but try to remember how happy you're making your children when you give them your undivided attention. Believe me, when they get older and start having lives of their own, you'll miss those long conversations about everyday details of their lives.

Give your child a great place of her own. Everyone needs to have her own little piece of the world. That's why adults work so hard to buy their first house. Let your child decorate her room. You might like a Victorian motif with soft pastel colors, but it isn't your room. Let your child pick the paint color, organize the furniture her way and hang her favorite posters on the wall. If your children have to share a room, let them each decorate their own space within the room.

The same is true for the rest of the home. Make sure your kids have a space where they can play and store some of their toys. You may want to keep an office area just for you, but overall, the house should be as much your child's as it is your own. I've never been fond of the idea of forbidding children from entering the living room or eating at the dining room table except for special occasions. Children are happiest when they live in a comfortable, family-focused home rather than in a museum designed for adults. Your children will grow up before you know it, and you'll have the rest of your life to turn your home into a more formal space (unless, like me, you hope to make it grandchild friendly someday).

Give your children surprises. Your children will have their whole lives to work hard and be responsible. Surprise them sometimes with little things. Consider adding their favorite desert in their lunch boxes, hiding a dollar under their pillows, throwing a surprise birthday party, telling them you're running errands and then take them to the zoo instead. Or invite several of their friends over for a surprise sleepover party. Babies love to be surprised during games of peek-a-boo and toddlers are thrilled when you bring out toys they haven't seen in a month or two. If you're a working parent, you can surprise your children by taking a day off of work and keeping them home from day care for a day of family fun.

Give children opportunities to be productive. Elderly people are teaching us the importance of feeling needed and being productive. Many adults who couldn't wait to retire are finding themselves eager to return to work after being out of the workforce for a short time. As much as we complain about work, we like to feel needed, to make a contribution, and to have others value what we do.

There are so many ways you can let your children contribute. Young kids love to help stir the brownie mix, set the table, rake the leaves (as best they can), or feed the goldfish. Older kids can help put socks on the baby, walk the dog, or wash some clothes. Make sure you thank your children for their help and let them know how much you appreciate it. Comments like, "Thanks for feeding the dog. I'm so tired tonight and that really helped" or "I don't know what I'd do without you. You're such a great help to me" go a long ways in helping your children feel like important members of the family.

Don't take your children's complaints about responsibilities too seriously, as long as you aren't giving them more than they can handle. Cut them a break when they're under a lot of stress. For example, your teen may complain about helping you cut firewood, but later you may hear him bragging to his peers about all the wood he cut.

Helping others is a great way to acquire satisfaction out of life. Sometimes your kids will talk about what they want as if they're the only people in the world. That egocentrism is normal. If you give your child opportunities to help others, however, he'll learn that making people smile can make him feel good as well.

Help your children become healthy. Your children aren't going to be happy if they feel tired from eating sugary snacks instead of a healthy dinner, have difficulty breathing due to lack of exercise, or are teased by peers because they're obese. Make living a healthy lifestyle a family project. Ask the kids to help plan and prepare healthy meals, encourage them to play sports, do yard work together as a family, and go for walks, ride bikes, or shoot baskets together.

Make family a priority. Make your holidays special by creating rituals such as opening Christmas presents on Christmas Eve every year or volunteering at the food kitchen every Thanksgiving. Try to make the holidays memorable. Decorate with cherished items or serve a dish or two that is a trademark of your family holidays. Every year on our Christmas tree we hang ornaments that have a place for a child's photo. The kids love searching through the ornament box to find pictures of themselves starting with their first Christmas.

Family should be a priority all year around, not just on holidays. Kids are happiest when they feel like they're an important part of your life. Try to have dinner together as a family, set aside time in the evening when you focus on your children instead of answering e-mails or talking on the phone, and keep work hours as reasonable as possible. Unfortunately, far too many parents look back on their lives and regret that they put their work before their children. Don't make that mistake with your kids.

Money doesn't buy happiness. If you're a happy person, material things may add to happiness. For example, if you enjoy boating, you may be happier when you buy a small lake house and can enjoy boating more often or no longer have to worry about putting your boat in and out of the water. But if you feel lonely, all the jewelry, expensive clothes, or luxury cars in the world won't make those sad feelings go away.

The same is true for your children. If your child feels loved, he will most likely feel happier, at least for a short time, if you buy him more of his favorite books or a few more of those model cars he loves to collect. However, if his father never shows up to take him for weekend visits, all the gifts in the world won't make him feel happy and loved.

Love your children with all your heart. If you really want to raise happy children, give them your unconditional love. That means—

- loving them even when you don't like what they're doing

- devoting your life to keeping them safe and well cared for
- nurturing them
- allowing them to become whomever they want to be
- making childhood a special time for them
- being there for them from the day they're born until you die.

Life isn't easy, but if your kids grow up feeling truly loved, they're likely to have a pretty, happy life.

Questions to Ponder

Did you have a happy childhood? Try to remember some of those happy times and then share some of those memories with your children. Think about those special times that you've never forgotten like a great family vacation or holiday rituals you loved most. Now think about some of those everyday activities that made you happy.

- Were there people in your life who made you feel loved or things you loved to do like playing with your dog, riding your bike with your best friend, or splashing in the pool?
- How are you doing with your children? Do you think they're happy, over all? If not, what can you do to make them happier?
- Do you need to try to work less, spend more time in play with them, or let them know how proud you are of them?
- Do you help them find happiness by having a purpose in life or helping others or do you try to buy them happiness?
- Do you let them be kids or do you take things too seriously and need to let them have more time in unstructured activities or just being silly?

CONCLUSION

I'm writing this last chapter as my oldest daughter, Rachel, prepares to leave home and venture out into the world. She graduated from high school two months ago and will be spending next year in France as a Rotary Exchange Student. She'll return the next summer, but then will head off to college the following fall.

This is a more difficult time than I had ever imagined it would be. I'm incredibly sad that Rachel's childhood is over, but I am so very proud of her. I know I'm biased, but I truly believe she has become a wonderful person.

I'm going to miss Rachel terribly, but I am very happy for her. I can't even imagine what she'll be like when she returns home after living with different families, assimilating to the French culture, and taking all of her courses, even Spanish, in French. I wish, when I was Rachel's age, I had found the courage to leave my comfort zone and do what she's doing.

I'm so glad Megan will be home for three more years. Lately, she's been asking me to go riding with her several days a week and my answer is usually "Yes." I know she'll be heading to college, too, before I know it, and I don't want to miss one minute of her childhood. I feel so fortunate she wants to spend quality time with me.

As I complete this book, I leave you with some final thoughts.

1. Cherish every moment.

Before you know it, like Rachel, your children will leave home. The years go by slowly when children are young but seem to fly by once they reach middle school. It can be hard to think about that when it's two in the morning, your baby won't go back to sleep, and you can't imagine how you're going to survive the next day. But cherish those moments when your baby just wants you to hold her and rock her to sleep, your toddler wants you to push her on the swing for what seems like hours, or your preteen wants to tell you every detail about her day at school because, before you know it, those opportunities will be gone.

2. Raising children can be a time of great personal growth for both you and your children.

So often we think about how our children are growing and changing and don't notice the changes in ourselves. If you stay flexible and open to learning new things, you'll find your children can teach you more than you ever imagined. They will make sure you take time out from the tasks of daily living to play, and they will remind you that relationships are what matter most in life. They'll introduce you to new activities and encourage you to step outside of your comfort zone. If you respond appropriately to their needs, your children will teach you to be more nurturing, patient, and flexible than you might have become if you hadn't decided to have children.

3. Build a relationship to last a lifetime.

Hopefully, you won't just *raise* your children, but you'll maintain a close and loving relationship with them throughout life. If you aren't too judgmental, they'll want to call you for advice. If you show genuine interest in their lives, they'll be anxious to talk with you about important events in their lives as they occur. Your relationship with your children will change over the years. Like all relationships, there will be times of tension and conflict. But if you treat your children with respect and kindness, they will remain close to you throughout your lifetime. What more could any of us ask?

4. Try to keep regrets to a minimum.

You are going to make mistakes with your children. It's inevitable. You'll need to learn to forgive yourself but also to take responsibility for your behavior. It's important, though, to remember you can't raise your children twice. If you don't nurture your children when they're young, you really can't make up for that later.

Too many people have looked back and regretted not being at a child's championship football game, failing to be there for their kids following a divorce, working long hours when their kids were young, or wishing they had been a little kinder, more supportive, or more patient. Keep those thoughts in the back of your mind and periodically ask yourself if you might have regrets after your children are grown. If you think you could do better, put your thoughts into action and be a better parent today. Most importantly, don't forget to place your children first. Once they're grown, you'll have plenty of time to focus on yourself again.

5. Remember that your job as a parent is to create a wonderful person.

Think about the type of person you'd like to have as

a friend, neighbor, coworker, or parent to your grand-children. As you watch the news at night and get frustrated by the state of the world, ask yourself what kind of people would make our world a better place. Then as you raise your children, think about the people you're creating. Make sure you give them a secure and loving childhood, teach them good values, help them find their passion, show them how to form loving relationships, and encourage them to try to make a positive impact on the lives of others. Remember, there's nothing more rewarding in life than to create wonderful people who will continue to make the world a better place to live long after you're gone.

I hope you enjoyed reading my book. I would love to hear about your experiences raising your children and look forward to communicating with you at—

www.creatingwonderfulpeople.com
or
creatingwonderfulpeople@gmail.com

— To Order —

Parents' Guide to
Creating Wonderful People:
How To Help Your Children Live
Happy and Meaningful Lives
by Jennifer Berryman, Ph.D.

If unavailable at your local bookstore,
place order to Dr. Jennifer Berryman
P.O. Box 281 • Little Meadows, PA 18830 or
on web site: www.creatingwonderfulpeople.com

— Or order directly from —
LangMarc Publishing • web site www.langmarc.com
or mail LangMarc • P.O. Box 90488
Austin, Texas 78709
Phone: 1-800-864-1648

Please send _____ copies of *Creating Wonderful People* to:

_____

_____

_____

$15.95 for 1 book + $3 shipping • 10% discount for 3-5
books + flat $4 shipping • 20% discount for 6 or more
books + flat $5 shipping. Checks or charge accepted.

Name/address on card bill:

_____

_____

_____

Card No: _____

Expiration date: _____ CVC Code: _____

CPSIA information can be obtained at www.ICGtesting.com
Printed in the USA
BVOW051714231011

274212BV00005B/4/P